Changes in Streamflow and the Flux of Nutrients in the Mississippi-Atchafalaya River Basin, USA, 1980–2007

By William A. Battaglin, Brent T. Aulenbach, Aldo Vecchia, and Herbert T. Buxton

Scientific Investigations Report 2009–5164

U.S. Department of the Interior
U.S. Geological Survey

U.S. Department of the Interior
KEN SALAZAR, Secretary

U.S. Geological Survey
Marcia K. McNutt, Director

U.S. Geological Survey, Reston, Virginia: 2010

For more information on the USGS—the Federal source for science about the Earth, its natural and living resources, natural hazards, and the environment, visit http://www.usgs.gov or call 1-888-ASK-USGS

For an overview of USGS information products, including maps, imagery, and publications, visit http://www.usgs.gov/pubprod

To order this and other USGS information products, visit http://store.usgs.gov

Suggested citation:
Battaglin, W.A., Aulenbach, B.T., Vecchia, A., and Buxton, H.T., 2010, Changes in streamflow and the flux of nutrients in the Mississippi-Atchafalaya River Basin, USA, 1980–2007: U.S. Geological Survey Scientific Investigations Report 2009–5164, Reston, Virginia, 48 p.

Contents

Figures

Tables

Conversion Factors

Multiply	By	To obtain
Length		
meter (m)	3.281	foot (ft)
kilometer (km)	0.6214	mile (mi)
Area		
square meter (m^2)	0.0002471	acre
square kilometer (km^2)	0.3861	square mile (mi^2)
Volume		
cubic meter (m^3)	264.2	gallon (gal)
cubic meter (m^3)	35.31	cubic foot (ft^3)
cubic meter (m^3)	0.0008107	acre-foot (acre-ft)
Flow rate		
cubic meter per second (m^3/s)	70.07	acre-foot per day (acre-ft/d)
cubic meter per second (m^3/s)	35.31	cubic foot per second (ft^3/s)
cubic meter per second (m^3/s)	22.83	million gallons per day (Mgal/d)
Mass		
kilogram (kg)	2.205	pound avoirdupois (lb)
metric ton (t)	1.102	ton, short (2,000 lb)
megagram (Mg)	1.102	ton, short (2,000 lb)
metric ton per year (t/y)	1.102	ton per year (ton/yr)

Temperature in degrees Celsius (°C) may be converted to degrees Fahrenheit (°F) as follows:

$$°F=(1.8×°C)+32$$

Vertical coordinate information is referenced to the North American Vertical Datum of 1988 (NAVD 88).

Horizontal coordinate information is referenced to the North American Datum of 1983 (NAD 83).

Altitude, as used in this report, refers to distance above the vertical datum.

Concentrations of chemical constituents in water are given in milligrams per liter (mg/L).

Changes in Streamflow and the Flux of Nutrients in the Mississippi-Atchafalaya River Basin, USA, 1980–2007

By William A. Battaglin, Brent T. Aulenbach, Aldo Vecchia, and Herbert T. Buxton

Abstract

Nutrients and freshwater delivered by the Mississippi and Atchafalaya Rivers drive algal production in the northern Gulf of Mexico, which eventually results in the widespread occurrence of hypoxic bottom waters along the Louisiana and Texas coast. Researchers have demonstrated a relation between the extent of the hypoxic zone and the magnitude of streamflow, nutrient fluxes, and nutrient concentrations in the Mississippi River, with springtime streamflows and fluxes being the most predictive. In 1999 the U.S. Geological Survey (USGS) estimated the flux of nitrogen, phosphorus, and silica at selected sites in the Mississippi Basin and to the Gulf of Mexico for 1980–1996. These flux estimates provided the baseline information used by the Mississippi River/Gulf of Mexico Watershed Nutrient Task Force to develop an Action Plan for reducing hypoxia in the northern Gulf of Mexico. The primary goal of the Action Plan was to achieve a reduction in the size (areal extent) of the hypoxic zone from an average of approximately 14,000 square kilometers in 1996–2000 to a 5-year moving average of less than 5,000 square kilometers by 2015.

Improved statistical models and adjusted maximum likelihood estimation using USGS Load Estimator (LOADEST) software were used to estimate annual and seasonal nutrient fluxes for 1980–2007 at selected sites on the Mississippi River and its tributaries. These data provide a means to evaluate the influence of natural and anthropogenic effects on delivery of water and nutrients to the Gulf of Mexico; to define subbasins that are the most important contributors of nutrients to the gulf; and to investigate the relations among streamflow, nutrient fluxes, and the size and duration of the Gulf of Mexico hypoxic zone. A comparative analysis between the baseline period of 1980–1996 and 5-year moving averages thereafter indicate that the average annual streamflow and fluxes of total nitrogen, nitrate, orthophosphate, and silica to the Gulf of Mexico have decreased. However, the flux of total phosphorus between the baseline period and subsequent 5-year periods has increased. The average spring (April, May, and June) streamflow and fluxes of silica, total nitrogen, nitrate, and orthophosphate to the Gulf of Mexico also decreased, whereas the spring flux of total phosphorus has increased. Similar changes in streamflow and nutrient flux were observed at many sites within the basin. The inputs of water, total nitrogen, and total phosphorus from the major subbasins of the Mississippi-Atchafalaya River Basin as a percentage of the to-the-gulf totals have increased from the Ohio River Basin, decreased from the Missouri River Basin, and remained relatively unchanged from the Upper Mississippi, Red, and Arkansas River Basins.

Changes in streamflow and nutrient fluxes are related, but short-term variations in sources of streamflow and nutrients complicate the interpretation of factors that affect nutrient delivery to the Gulf of Mexico. Parametric time-series models are used to try and separate natural variability in nutrient flux from changes due to other causes. Results indicate that the decrease in annual nutrient fluxes that has occurred between the 1980–1996 baseline period and more recent years can be largely attributed to natural causes (climate and streamflow) and not management actions or other human controlled activities in the Mississippi-Atchafalaya River Basin. The downward trends in total nitrogen, nitrate, ammonium, and orthophosphate that were detected at either the Mississippi River near St. Francisville, La., or the Atchafalaya River at Melville, La., occurred prior to 1995.

In spite of the general decrease in nutrient flux, the average size of the Gulf of Mexico hypoxic zone has increased between 1997 and 2007. The reasons for this are not clear but could be due to the type or nature of nutrient delivery. Whereas the annual flux of total nitrogen to the Gulf of Mexico has decreased, the proportion of that flux that is nitrate steadily increased from about 55 percent in the 1980s to about 70 percent in recent years.

Introduction

The Mississippi and Atchafalaya Rivers drain an area of greater than 3,000,000 km^2 or about 41 percent of the conterminous United States (fig. 1) including parts or all of 30 States extending from the Appalachians to the Rocky Mountains. The Mississippi-Atchafalaya River Basin (MARB) is one of the most productive farming regions in the world. Much of the agricultural production in the MARB relies on the use of agricultural chemicals: pesticides and chemical fertilizers.

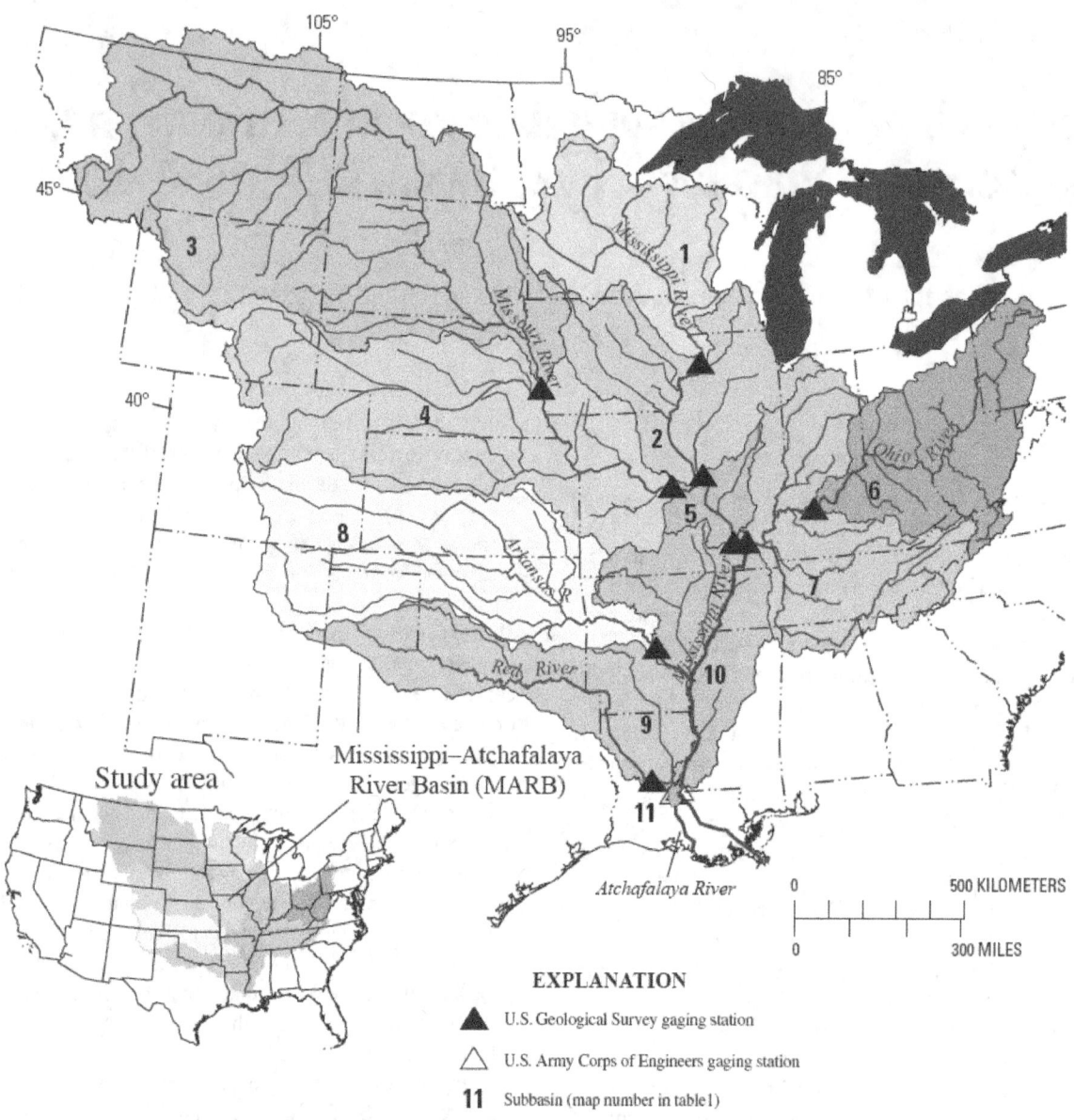

Figure 1.   Locations of sites used for nutrient flux estimates and associated large subbasins.

For example, about 7 million metric tons of nitrogen in commercial fertilizers is applied annually in the basin (Goolsby and Battaglin, 2000; Ruddy and others, 2006). However, crop production is not the only source of nutrients in the MARB. The basin is home to more than 76 million people (U.S. Census Bureau, 2008) who produce nutrient wastes that are often treated and discharged by wastewater treatment plants. The basin also is the rearing ground for approximately 57 million cattle, 40 million pigs, and 565 million chickens and turkeys (Ruddy and others, 2006) and the home of a large number of industries that discharge nutrients in their wastewater.

Previous studies have shown that runoff and groundwater from the basin can contain elevated amounts of nutrients, such as nitrate and orthophosphate (Goolsby and others, 1993, 1999; Kolpin and others, 1993; Meade, 1995; U.S. Geological Survey, 1999). Some of these nutrients are transported to streams, then to the Mississippi River, and eventually to the Gulf of Mexico. Modeling studies (Booth and Campbell, 2007; Alexander and others, 2008) indicate that in general, fertilizer use on crops is the primary source of nitrogen (N), and animal manure is the primary source of phosphorus (P). The bulk of both the N and P originate from watersheds draining parts of nine States: Arkansas, Illinois, Indiana, Iowa, Kentucky, Mississippi, Missouri, Ohio, and Tennessee. However, the models do not account for annual variability or changes in climate, changes in cropping practices, implementation of farming best management practices (BMPs), urbanization, or other processes or incentives that reduce nutrient inputs to the land surface or directly to streams.

Inputs of nutrients from agricultural and other sources have caused phytoplankton blooms and the formation of hypoxic zones in near-shore oceanic environments worldwide (Diaz and Rosenberg, 2008). Nutrients and freshwater delivered by the Mississippi and Atchafalaya Rivers drive algal production in the northern Gulf of Mexico, which eventually results in the widespread occurrence of hypoxic (containing less than 2 mg/L of dissolved oxygen) bottom waters along the Louisiana and Texas coast (Rabalais and others, 1999, 2002, 2007; U.S Environmental Protection Agency, 2007). Recently, researchers have modeled the extent of the hypoxic zone as a function of streamflow, nutrient fluxes, or nutrient concentrations (Scavia and others, 2004; Donner and Scavia, 2007; Scavia and Donnelly, 2007; Turner and others, 2008; Boesch and others, 2009). These models all indicate that there is a strong positive correlation between nitrogen and(or) phosphorus flux to the Gulf of Mexico and the size of the hypoxic zone. Several of the models indicate that the springtime flux is most influential in determining the size of the hypoxic zone. Some of these studies indicate that the relation between nutrient flux and the size of the hypoxic zone is changing and that the Gulf of Mexico is becoming more susceptible to nutrient inputs (Stow and others, 2005; Turner and others, 2008).

Purpose and Scope

The purpose of this report is to document streamflow conditions and estimates of the fluxes of nutrients (dissolved nitrite plus nitrate (nitrate), total organic nitrogen plus ammonia nitrogen (TKN), dissolved ammonia, total phosphorus (TP), dissolved orthophosphate (OP), and dissolved silica) to the Gulf of Mexico from both the Atchafalaya and mainstem Mississippi Rivers. The report also documents streamflow and flux estimates for 9 other major subbasins and 21 smaller subbasins within the MARB. Specifically, streamflow and flux estimates from 1980 through 1996, as previously reported (Goolsby and others, 1999), are compared with 5-year moving average values for 1997 through 2006 (and in some cases 2007). By making these comparisons, this report addresses task 11 from the Hypoxia Action Plan (Mississippi River/Gulf of Mexico Watershed Nutrient Task Force, 2001), which states in part that "By December 2005, and every 5 years thereafter, the Task Force will assess the nutrient load reductions achieved and the response of the hypoxic zone." Also, the summaries of streamflow and flux from sites within the MARB will provide part of the information needed for determining the status of the second Environmental Indicator from the Hypoxia Action Plan, "seasonal/annual average

nitrogen and phosphorus concentrations and mass loadings are reduced at key river and tributary stations." This report follows the general format of Goolsby and others (1999) but does not include extensive discussions about nutrient sources, atmospheric deposition, or nutrient budgets.

Objectives

The objective of this report is to identify changes or trends in streamflow and nutrient fluxes to the Gulf of Mexico and at selected sites within the MARB for 1980 through 2006 (and in some cases 2007). Specific comparisons will be made between average values from 1980–1996, which are considered as baseline conditions for this report, and 5-year moving average values for 1997 through 2006. Trend analysis will be used to determine if any changes identified in the fluxes of nitrogen, phosphorus, and silica to the Gulf of Mexico reflect human influences such as changes in soil and nutrient management practices or crop planting patterns or are the result of changing natural conditions such as natural climatic variability. Finally, recent changes in streamflow and nutrient flux will be compared with changes in the size of the hypoxic zone to determine how the Gulf of Mexico is reacting to inputs from the MARB.

Study Sites

Since the mid-1970s the USGS National Stream Quality Accounting Network (NASQAN) program has measured nutrient concentrations in rivers of the United States. Over the years the number of sites, the number of constituents measured, and frequency of sample collection have changed to meet the changing objectives of the program. However, to a large extent, the overall intent of the program has remained consistent and is most simply stated as "accounting for the quantity and quality of water moving within and from the United States" (Ficke and Hawkinson, 1975). Since the mid-1980s, estimation of mass transport (flux) of selected constituents has been a primary NASQAN objective. Most study sites used for this study were or are operated by the USGS NASQAN program, but some sites were or are operated by the USGS National Water-Quality Assessment Program (NAWQA) or by individual USGS Water Science Centers, and these sites may have operated with different program objectives.

In this report, streamflow and nutrient flux estimates for 1980-2007 are summarized for 33 sites in the MARB. Eleven sites (fig. 1, table 1) are located on the Mississippi River main stem and many of its largest tributaries. These sites generally coincide with the large basin sites from Goolsby and others (1999). Most of these sites have complete sets of nutrient-concentration data for the 1980 to 2006 time period, although for some sites, as many as 10 years of data are missing from this period (table 1). Twenty-one sites (fig. 2, table 2) are located on generally smaller rivers within the MARB. Many

Table 1. Site names, site identification numbers, drainage areas, subbasin numbers and period of record for total nitrogen flux estimates at 11 sites on the Mississippi and Atchafalaya Rivers and their major tributaries. [ID, site identification number; subbasin number column refers to the subbasins identified on figure 1; km², square kilometers].

Site Name	ID	Drainage area (km²)	Subbasin number(s)	Period of record (for total nitrogen)
Mississippi River at Clinton, Iowa	05420500	222,000	1	1975–1987, 1996–2006
Mississippi River below Grafton, Ill.[1]	05587455	443,700	1, 2	1975–1994, 1996–2006
Missouri River at Omaha, Nebr.	06610000	836,000	3	1978–1986, 1996–2006
Missouri River at Hermann, Mo.	06934500	1,353,000	3, 4	1973–2006
Mississippi River at Thebes, Ill.	07022000	1,847,000	1, 2, 3, 4, 5	1973–2006
Ohio River at Cannelton Dam at Cannelton, Ind.	03303280	251,000	6	1976–1986, 1996–2006
Ohio River at Dam 53 near Grand Chain, Ill[2]	03612500	526,000	6, 7	1973–2006
Arkansas River below Little Rock, Ark.	07263620	409,960	8	1972–2006
Red River at Alexandria, La.	07355500	175,000	9	1973–2006
Mississippi River near St. Francisville, La.[3]	07373420	2,967,000	1, 2, 3, 4, 5, 6, 7, 8, 10	1975–2007
Atchafalaya River at Melville, La.[4]	07381495	241,700	9, 11	1980–2007

[1] Flow from Mississippi River at Grafton, Ill. (05587500). Data prior to 1989 are from the Mississippi at Alton, IL (05587500) and Mississippi below Alton, Ill. (05587550).

[2] Flow from Ohio River at Metropolis, Ill. (03611500).

[3] Flow from Mississippi River at Tarbert Landing, Miss. (U.S. Army Corps of Engineers site 01100).

[4] Flow from Atchafalaya River at Simmesport, La. (U.S. Army Corps of Engineers site 03045).

of these sites coincide with the 42 interior basin sites from Goolsby and others (1999). Nutrient concentration data from these sites are much less complete with only a few sites having a complete or near complete record for the 1980 to 2006 time period (table 2). Other sites that were included in the 42 interior basins from Goolsby's report are not included in this report because water-quality data were lacking or insufficient to calculate flux estimates for recent years.

Methods

Water-Quality Samples

All water-quality samples used in this analysis were collected by the USGS using consistent protocols (U.S. Geological Survey, variously dated) as described in Aulenbach and others (2007). Water-quality analyses for nutrients were conducted by USGS laboratories, and data from these analyses are stored in the USGS National Water Information System (NWIS) database. The water-quality samples were collected principally by the USGS NASQAN program, but some samples collected by the USGS National Water-Quality Assessment Program (NAWQA) or by individual USGS Water Science Centers also are used. Quality assurance and quality

control (QA/QC) sample associated with the data summarized in this report are stored in the USGS National Water Information System (NWIS) database and were collected following NASQAN program protocols (Kelly and others, 2001).

Over the period of study, changes in field and analytical methods have resulted in changes to the laboratory reporting levels for some nutrients and in some cases changes to the number and types of nutrients analyzed for (Goolsby and others, 1999). Prior to use in the flux models, the nutrient-concentration data sets were screened for errors, outliers, duplicate samples, and quality-assurance samples (for details see Aulenbach and others, 2007).

Streamflow data for all sites in this study were obtained from the USGS NWIS database (*http://waterdata.usgs.gov/co/nwis/rt/*), the U.S. Army Corps of Engineers New Orleans District Water Control Section Website (*http://www.mvn.usace.army.mil/eng/edhd/watercon.asp*), or the Tennessee Valley Authority (*http://www.tva.gov/*).

Flux Calculation Methods

The annual and monthly transport (flux) to the Gulf of Mexico of several nutrients was reported by Goolsby and others (1999) and has recently been reported each year on a USGS Web site for selected locations (U.S. Geological

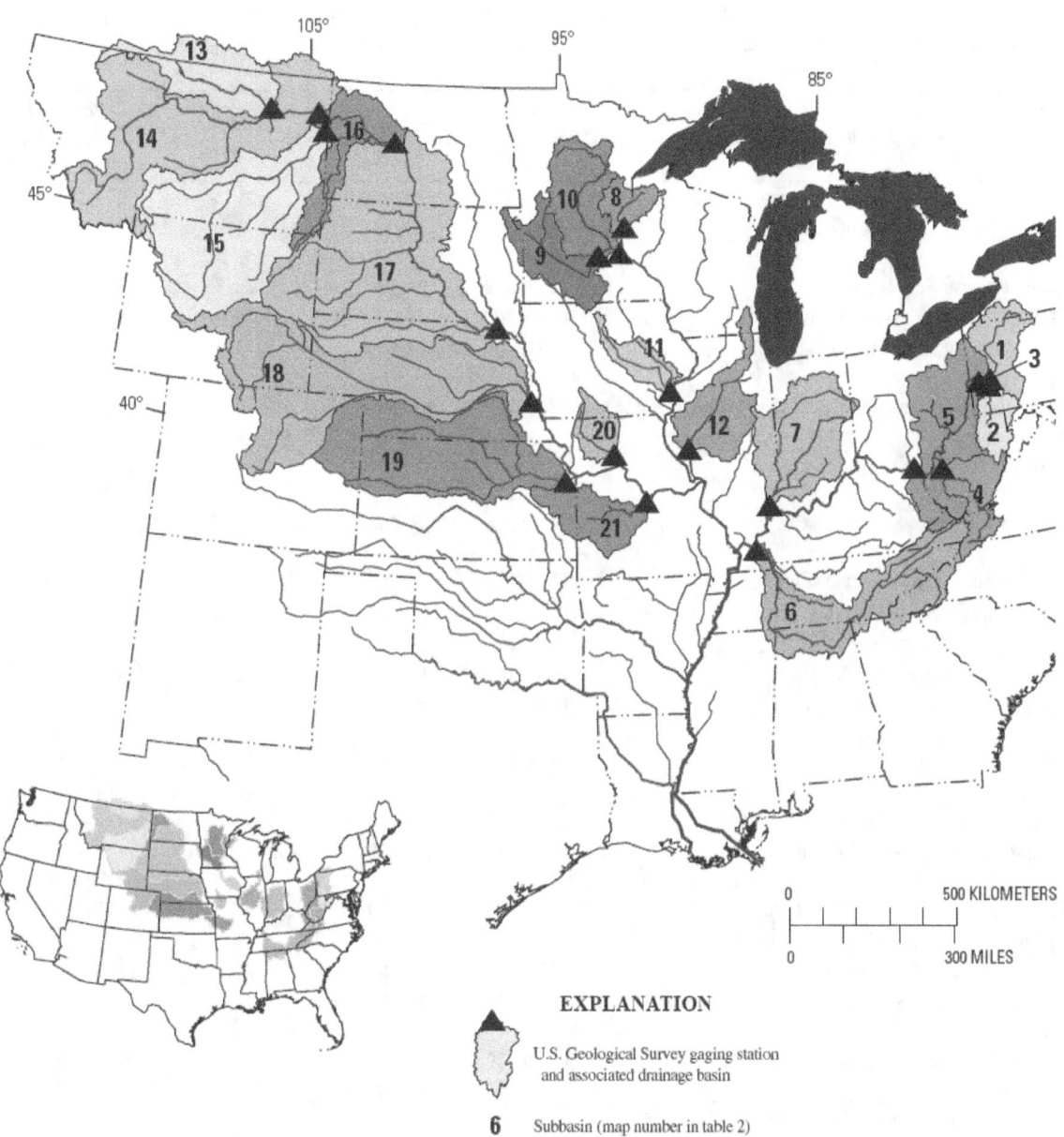

Figure 2. Locations of sites used for nutrient flux estimates and associated small subbasins.

Table 2.   Site names, site identification numbers, drainage areas, subbasin numbers and period of record for total nitrogen flux estimates at 21 sites within the Mississippi-Atchafalaya River Basin used for nutrient flux estimation. [ID, site identification number; subbasin number column refers to the subbasins identified on figure 2; km², square kilometers]

Site name	ID	Drainage area (km²)	Subbasin number(s)	Period of record (for total nitrogen)
Allegheny River at New Kensington, Pa.[1]	03049625	29,900	1	1973–2000
Monongahela R at Braddock, Pa.	03085000	19,000	2	1973–1993, 1995–2000
Ohio River at Sewickley, Pa.	03086000	50,500	1, 2, 3	2001–2006
Kanawha River at Winfield, W. Va.[2]	03201300	30,600	4	1974–1995
Ohio River at Greenup Dam near Greenup, Ky.	03216600	161,000	1, 2, 3, 4, 5	1975–1986, 1997–2006
Tennessee River at Highway 60 near Paducah, Ky.[3]	03609750	104,500	6	1974–1986, 1997–2006
Wabash River at New Harmony, Ind.[4]	03378500	75,700	7	1975–1982, 1997–2006
St. Croix River at St. Croix Falls, Wis.	05340500	16,200	8	1975–1986, 1996–2001
Minnesota River at Jordan, Minn.	05330000	42,000	9	1973–1998
Mississippi River at Hastings, Minn.[5]	05331580	96,100	9, 10	1996–2004
Iowa River at Wapello, Iowa	05465500	32,400	11	1978–2003
Illinois River at Valley City, Ill.	05586100	69,300	12	1975–2004
Milk River near Nashua, Mont.	06174500	57,800	13	1974–1994, 1999–2003
Missouri River near Culbertson, Mont.	06185500	237,100	13, 14	1975–1984, 1997–2006
Yellowstone River near Sidney, Mont.	06329500	178,900	15	1973–2003
Missouri River at Garrison Dam, N. Dak.	06338490	469,800	13, 14, 15, 16	1974–1995, 1997–2006
Missouri River at Yankton, S. Dak.	06467500	723,900	13, 14, 15, 16, 17	2001–2005
Platte River at Louisville, Nebr.	06805500	221,000	18	1975–2003
Kansas River at DeSoto, Kans.	06892350	154,800	19	1975–1991
Grand River near Sumner, Mo.	06902000	17,800	20	1968–1997, 1999–2006
Osage River below St. Thomas, Mo.[6]	06926510	37,800	21	1975–1997, 1999–2006

[1]Flow from Allegheny River at Natrona, Pa. (03049500).

[2]Flow from Kanawha River at Charleston, W. Va. (03198000).

[3]Flow from Tennessee River near Paducah, Ky. (03609500).

[4]Flow from Wabash River at Mt. Carmel, Ill. (03377500).

[5]Flow from Mississippi River at St Paul, Minn. (05331000).

[6]Flow prior to 1997 from Osage River near St. Thomas, Mo. (06926500).

Survey, 2009; Aulenbach and others, 2007). These data have been used extensively by researchers interested in the formation of hypoxia in the Gulf of Mexico (Rabalais and others, 1999; Goolsby and others, 1999, Goolsby and Battaglin, 2001; Scavia and others, 2004; Booth and Campbell, 2007; Donner and Scavia, 2007; Turner and others, 2008) and are currently the foundation for many management decisions related to the hypoxia problem (Committee on Environment and Natural Resources, 2000, 2003; Mississippi River/Gulf of Mexico Watershed Nutrient Task Force, 2001, 2004; U.S. Environmental Protection Agency, 2008).

The original nutrient-flux estimates were calculated using standard regression-model techniques (Cohn and others, 1992; Goolsby and others, 1999) and included terms for daily average streamflow (log of streamflow and streamflow-squared), season (sine and cosine of day-of-year), and time (both time and time-squared). At some large-river sites, streamflow values from upstream sites were included because these values better described the variations in concentrations. The regression models were typically calibrated for the entire period of study, with the exception of some of the large river sites with longer periods of record for which the study period was sometimes split into two calibration periods for selected constituents. When nutrient concentrations were below the laboratory reporting level, one-half the laboratory reporting level was substituted into the calculations. When 20 percent or more of samples from a site had nutrient concentrations below the laboratory reporting level, a streamflow-weighted average method was used to calculate flux estimates (Goolsby and others, 1999). Total nitrogen (TN) fluxes were estimated directly from a calibration dataset of TN concentrations created by summing sample dissolved nitrate and TKN concentrations. Annual flux estimates were made and reported for the calendar year (January 1 through December 31).

In 2002, a new method (Aulenbach and others, 2007) was applied to estimate nutrient fluxes for the lower Mississippi River and Atchafalaya River sites (to determine the nutrient delivery to the Gulf of Mexico), which produced similar, but not identical estimates of nutrient flux as had been reported earlier. The new flux estimates were calculated using the same model (ESTIMATOR; Cohn and others, 1992) used by Goolsby and others (1999), but the model structure and calibration periods were changed. The newer models did not include a time-squared term and used different upstream streamflow terms for the lower Mississippi River site in order to improve model performance. The model-calibration period (a 10-year moving period) also differed from that in the Goolsby and others (1999) report. Flow terms from upstream sites (Mississippi River at Thebes, Ill., and Ohio River at Dam 53 near Grand Chain, Ill.) were used in addition to onsite streamflows for the lower Mississippi River model. Upstream streamflows were lagged 10 days to account for travel time between the upstream and downstream sites (Moody, 1993). TN fluxes were not determined by a separate model, but were calculated by summing independently estimated dissolved

nitrate and TKN fluxes. Annual flux estimates were made and reported for the water year (October 1 of the previous year through September 30 of the designated year) and not the calendar year.

The nutrient-flux estimates summarized in this report were calculated with a regression-model method using Load Estimator (LOADEST), a FORTRAN-based load (or flux) estimation program (Runkel and others, 2004). LOADEST estimates fluxes using various algorithms including adjusted maximum-likelihood estimates (AMLE) for different statistical distributions of the data and applies correction factors for transformation-bias corrections from a log model back to linear space. AMLE results are used in this study. The AMLE approach handles censored water-quality data (concentrations below the reporting level) by inferring the censored sample concentrations from the statistical distribution of sample concentrations above the reporting level. A complete description of the data and models used to estimate nutrient fluxes in the MARB is provided by Aulenbach and others (2007).

At some sites, regression models failed to explain a significant portion of the variance in observed nutrient concentrations and, hence, nutrient flux. The models generally failed to accurately predict concentration during extreme events, and in general the residuals between predicted and observed daily flux estimates were not random, but showed patterns (residuals were serially autocorrelated). These errors were not particularly significant when using the model to develop annual flux estimates, but they are of more concern for monthly flux estimates, which increasingly are being used by Gulf of Mexico hypoxia researchers.

Nutrient Inputs

Estimates of the annual nitrogen (N) and phosphorus (P) inputs from both point and nonpoint sources were reported by Goolsby and others (1999), and others have recently generated or used similar sets of nutrient-input information (Booth and Campbell, 2007; Alexander and others, 2008). For this report, county-level estimates of N and P inputs from fertilizer, animal manure, industrial and municipal point sources, and atmospheric deposition for 1980–2004 were obtained from various sources (Alexander and Smith, 1990; Battaglin and Goolsby, 1995; Ruddy and others, 2006; Mississippi River/Gulf of Mexico Watershed Nutrient Task Force, 2006). Inputs from soil mineralization are not addressed in this report but have been addressed by others (Burkart and James, 1999). A geographic information system (GIS) was used to manage the county-level information for N and P inputs, and an area-weighted sum algorithm programmed in the GIS (Battaglin and Goolsby, 1998) was used to estimate the inputs of N and P within drainage basins associated with the sampling sites (figs. 1 and 2). The algorithm accounts for cases where an entire county is within a single drainage basin and where only a portion of a county is within a drainage basin.

Statistical Methods

Statistics are used for two general purposes in this report. First, comparisons are made between average values for the baseline period (1980 through 1996) and 5-year moving averages for 1997 through 2007. Second, an analysis is conducted to indentify natural variability and human-caused trends in the data for 1980–2006.

Comparison of Baseline to Recent Conditions

In most cases in this report, comparisons between baseline and recent conditions are made by calculating the percent difference between the mean values as shown in equation 1. However, for some constituents (for example, orthophosphate) and at some sites, the periods of record differ. Means were not calculated and percent differences were not reported when one-half or more of the annual (or spring) flux estimates were missing.

$$[(1980\text{–}1996 \text{ mean} - 5\text{-year mean})/1980\text{–}1996 \text{ mean}] \quad (1)$$
$$\times 100 = \text{percent difference}$$

More rigorous methods are required to determine if the observed differences are statistically significant. As described earlier and in the Action Plans (Mississippi River/Gulf of Mexico Watershed Nutrient Task Force, 2001, 2008), progress toward a goal of reduced hypoxia and subsequent evaluations of management decisions are to be determined by comparing 1980–1996 average nutrient flux; hence, the mean of 17 values, with 5-year moving average fluxes (each are the mean of five values) for 1997 to the present. This creates some difficulty statistically as standard tests for differences in means between two or more populations generally depend on the populations having normal distributions, equal variance, or at least large sample size. The nutrient-flux data set does not satisfy any of these assumptions. Hence, a nonparametric statistic, the Kruskal-Wallis test (Helsel and Hirsch, 2002), is used to determine if the medians of the populations are different. However, the comparison of median values instead of mean values does not exactly address the needs of the Action Plan.

Trend Analysis

Nutrient fluxes from four major subbasins are statistically analyzed for trends in an effort to distinguish human influenced changes in nutrient flux from inherent natural variability. The four subbasins selected for statistical trend analysis include: the Mississippi River near St. Francisville, La., the Atchafalaya River at Melville, La., the Ohio River at Dam 53 near Grand Chain, Ill., and the Mississippi River at Thebes, Ill. Trends in annual streamflows and nutrient fluxes are analyzed first, using standard statistical techniques, and then a more powerful time-series model is used to analyze trends in daily flux.

The first statistical analysis is based on the annual streamflows and nutrient-flux estimates, previously described, in which the Kruskal-Wallis (KW) test is used to test for a significant difference between the annual streamflow and nutrient fluxes for the baseline (1980–1996) period and the recent (2000–2006) period. A significant result for the KW test for annual nutrient fluxes indicates that the fluxes have changed but does not indicate how much of the change may have been due to changing streamflow conditions. To determine if the trends in annual nutrient fluxes may have been due, at least in part, to changing annual streamflow conditions, a second KW test was done using the residuals from a linear regression of annual nutrient flux on annual streamflow. Comparison of the test results for the residuals with the test results for the unadjusted fluxes indicated that variable streamflow conditions had a substantial influence on the unadjusted trends in nutrient fluxes.

To better separate natural variability from variability due to other causes, a parametric time-series model (Vecchia, 2005) was used. The time-series model was developed for jointly estimating trends in streamflow and chemical concentration data using a 10-day time step. Although the model was developed using concentration data, it is applicable for analyzing trends in flux as well. However, because of the complexity of the model, methods for using the model to obtain unbiased estimates of annual fluxes similar to the AMLE method are not yet available. Therefore, the fluxes computed using the time-series model were not converted to annual flux estimates and are not reported here.

For the time series analysis, each month of the study period (1980–2006) was divided into three approximately 10-day intervals (the 1st through the 10th day of the month, the 11th through the 20th, and the 21th through the end of the month). For intervals with at least one concentration sample, the average daily flux for the interval was computed by multiplying the concentration from the sample nearest to the midpoint of the interval times the average daily streamflow for the interval. For intervals with no concentration samples, the missing average daily flux for the interval was estimated from the time-series model using a Kalman filtering algorithm (Vecchia, 2005) and the non-missing streamflow and flux values.

The model structure is briefly described here. For more detail, refer to Appendix 1 from Vecchia (2005). Log-transformed streamflow and nutrient flux for each 10-day interval are expressed as:

$$\log Q(t) = M_Q + ANN_Q + SEAS_Q + HFV_Q \quad (2)$$
and
$$\log F(t) = M_F + ANN_F + SEAS_F + TREND_F + HFV_F \quad (3)$$

where

log denotes the base-10 logarithm;
t denotes a particular 10-day time interval;
$Q(t)$ is average streamflow for interval t, in cubic meters per second;

$F(t)$ is estimated average daily flux for interval
  t, in metric tons per day;
M_Q (M_F) is the long-term logarithmic mean for
  streamflow (flux);
ANN_Q (ANN_F) is the annual anomaly for streamflow
  (flux);
$SEAS_Q$ ($SEAS_F$) is the seasonal anomaly for
  streamflow (flux);
HFV_Q (HFV_F) is high-frequency variability for
  streamflow (flux); and
$TREND_F$ is a long-term trend in flux.

The annual anomalies for both streamflow and flux
are functions of the streamflow values for 5 years up to
and including time t, and represent long-term (interannual)
variability in streamflow and long-term streamflow-related
variability in flux. The seasonal anomalies for streamflow and
flux represent seasonal variability in streamflow and seasonal
streamflow-related variability in flux. The high-frequency variability for both streamflow and flux represents short-term deviations from the annual and seasonal anomalies and includes
serial correlation, cross-correlation, and standard deviations
that depend on the time of year. The trend represents the long-
term changes in flux that are not related to streamflow and,
thus, presumably reflect changes in land use, fertilizer appli-
cation, or other factors. A trend term for streamflow could be
included as well; however, for this analysis, potential trends
in streamflow were combined with the annual anomaly, and
only trends in flux were evaluated. The trend in flux consists
of piecewise monotonic trends for specified time intervals that
are selected empirically on the basis of generalized likelihood
ratio tests as described by Vecchia (2005, Appendix 1).

Streamflow and Nutrient Flux in the Mississippi-Atchafalaya River Basin

Summaries of the model results are provided in a series
of figures and tables. Streamflow and nutrient flux results are
divided into three categories: (1) to the Gulf of Mexico, (2) in
11 major subbasins of the MARB, and (3) in 21 smaller subbasins. In the data tables, summaries of streamflow and nutrient

flux are presented for the baseline period (1980–1996) and for
the last three or four 5-year periods, which in most cases are
2000–2004, 2001–2005, 2002–2006, and 2003–2007. Results
of KW tests for differences in median fluxes between the
baseline period and 5-year moving periods from 1997–2007
are provided only in the text. Estimates of the 95-percent
confidence intervals for the annual and monthly nutrient-flux
estimates summarized here are reported by Aulenbach and
others (2007). The annual and monthly nutrient flux estimates
at a site often are not independent, and the confidence limits
of these estimates cannot be added or averaged over multiyear
periods in a statistically valid way.

Fluxes to the Gulf of Mexico

Two sites are used to determine the streamflow and nutrient flux delivered to the Gulf of Mexico: (1) the Mississippi
River near St. Francisville, La., and (2) the Atchafalaya River
at Melville, La. Neither of these sites is very near to the actual
mouths of these rivers, but they were selected because they are
not influenced by the tidal cycle. Also, there are no significant
tributaries to the Mississippi River downstream from St. Francisville, nor are there any significant tributaries to the Atchafalaya River downstream from Melville. Approximately 30
percent of the flow of the Mississippi River is diverted into the
Atchafalaya River, upstream from the site near St. Francisville
(Aulenbach and others, 2007).

Streamflow

The estimated mean annual streamflow from the MARB
to the Gulf of Mexico for the 1980–1996 baseline period
was 21,940 m^3/s (table 3). The 5-year average mean annual
streamflow for 2001–2005 was 20,680 m^3/s, a 6-percent
decrease from the baseline period average. The 5-year average
mean annual streamflow for 2002–2006 was 19,440 m^3/s, an
11-percent decrease from the baseline period average. The
5-year average mean annual streamflow for 2003–2007 was
18,880 m^3/s, a 14-percent decrease from the baseline period
average. The seven 5-year average mean annual streamflows
for 1997–2007 were all less than the mean annual streamflow
for the baseline period and were on average less by 10 percent

Table 3. Mean annual and mean spring (April, May, June) streamflow from the Mississippi-Atchafalaya River Basin to
the Gulf of Mexico, 1980–1996, 2000–2004, 2001–2005, 2002–2006, and 2003–2007. [Subbasin number column refers to the
subbasins identified in figure 1; (m^3/s), cubic meters per second]

Subbasin numbers	Streamflow type	Stream-flow, (m^3/s)				
		1980–1996	2000–2004	2001–2005	2002–2006	2003–2007
1 to 11	Mean annual streamflow to the Gulf of Mexico	21,940	18,940	20,680	19,440	18,880
1 to 11	Mean spring streamflow to the Gulf of Mexico	30,110	26,650	26,800	25,000	22,230

(fig. 3). Median annual streamflows for the seven 5-year periods were not significantly different (p=0.72) from the median annual streamflow for the baseline period.

The estimated mean spring (April, May, and June) streamflow from the MARB to the Gulf of Mexico for the 1980–1996 baseline period was 30,110 m³/s (table 3); hence, approximately 34 percent of the total annual streamflow occurred during these 3 months. The 5-year average mean spring streamflow for 2002–2006 was 25,000 m³/s, a 17-percent decrease from the baseline period average. The 5-year average mean spring streamflow for 2003–2007 was 22,230 m³/s, a 26-percent decrease from the baseline period average. The seven 5-year average mean spring streamflows for 1997–2007 were all less than the mean spring streamflow for the baseline period and were on average less by 12 percent (fig. 4). Median spring streamflows for the seven 5-year periods were not significantly different (p=0.17) from the median spring streamflow for the baseline period.

Silica

The estimated mean annual flux of silica (as SiO_2) from the MARB to the Gulf of Mexico for the 1980–1996 baseline period is 4,531,200 metric tons (t) (table 4). The 5-year average mean annual silica flux for 2001–2005 was 3,814,000 t, a 16-percent decrease from the baseline period average. The 5-year average mean annual silica flux for 2002–2006 was 3,534,000 t, a 22-percent decrease from the baseline period average. The 5-year average mean annual silica flux for 2003–2007 was 3,714,000 t, an 18-percent decrease from the baseline period average. The seven moving 5-year average mean annual silica fluxes for 1997–2007 were all less than the mean annual silica flux for the baseline period and were on average less by 18 percent (fig. 3). Median annual silica fluxes for the seven 5-year periods were not significantly different (p=0.11) from the median silica flux for the baseline period.

The estimated mean spring silica flux from the MARB to the Gulf of Mexico for the 1980–1996 baseline period was 1,518,900 t (506,300 metric tons per month) (table 5); hence, on average, approximately 34 percent of the total silica flux occurred during these 3 months. The 5-year average mean spring silica flux for 2002–2006 was 1,078,500 t (359,500 t per month), a 29-percent decrease from the baseline period average. The 5-year average mean spring silica flux for 2003–2007 was 1,028,700 t (342,900 t per month), a 32-percent decrease from the baseline period average. The seven moving 5-year average mean spring silica fluxes for 1997–2007 were all less than the mean spring silica flux for the baseline period and were on average less by 20 percent (fig. 4). Median spring silica flux for at least one of the seven 5-year periods was significantly different (p=0.005) from the median spring silica flux for the baseline period.

Total Nitrogen

The estimated mean annual flux of total nitrogen as N (TN) from the MARB to the Gulf of Mexico for the 1980–1996 baseline period is 1,575,200 t (table 4). The 5-year average mean annual TN flux for 2001–2005 was 1,242,800 t, a 21-percent decrease from the baseline period average. The 5-year average mean annual TN flux for 2002–2006 was 1,146,200 t, a 27-percent decrease from the baseline period average. The 5-year average mean annual TN flux for 2003–2007 was 1,166,400 t, a 26-percent decrease from the baseline period average. The seven 5-year average mean annual TN fluxes for 1997–2007 were all less than the mean annual TN flux for the baseline period and were on average less by 23 percent (fig. 3). Median annual TN flux for at least one of the seven 5-year periods was significantly different (p=0.05) from the median TN flux for the baseline period.

The estimated mean spring TN flux from the MARB to the Gulf of Mexico for the 1980–1996 baseline period was 588,300 t (196,100 t per month) (table 5); hence, on average, approximately 37 percent of the TN flux occurred during these 3 months. The 5-year average mean spring TN flux for 2002–2006 was 432,900 t (144,300 t per month), a 26-percent decrease from the baseline period average. The 5-year average mean spring TN flux for 2003–2007 was 425,400 t (141,800 t per month), a 28-percent decrease from the baseline period average. The seven 5-year average mean spring TN fluxes for 1997–2007 were all less than the mean spring TN flux for the baseline period and were on average less by 18 percent (fig. 4). Median spring TN flux for at least one of the seven 5-year periods was significantly different (p=0.006) from the median spring TN flux for the baseline period.

Nitrate

The estimated mean annual flux of nitrate plus nitrite as N (nitrate) from the MARB to the Gulf of Mexico for the 1980–1996 baseline period is 961,500 t (table 4). The 5-year average mean annual nitrate flux for 2001–2005 was 813,400 t, a 15-percent decrease from the baseline period average. The 5-year average mean annual nitrate flux for 2002–2006 was 757,000 t, a 21-percent decrease from the baseline period average. The 5-year average mean annual nitrate flux for 2003–2007 was 779,000 t, a 19-percent decrease from the baseline period average. The seven 5-year average mean annual nitrate fluxes for 1997–2007 were all less than the mean annual nitrate flux for the baseline period and were on average less by 15 percent (fig. 3). The annual flux of nitrate as a percentage of the TN flux increased from 61 percent during the baseline period to 67 percent during the 2003–2007 5-year period (table 4). Median annual nitrate fluxes for the seven 5-year periods were not significantly different (p=0.23) from the median nitrate flux for the baseline period.

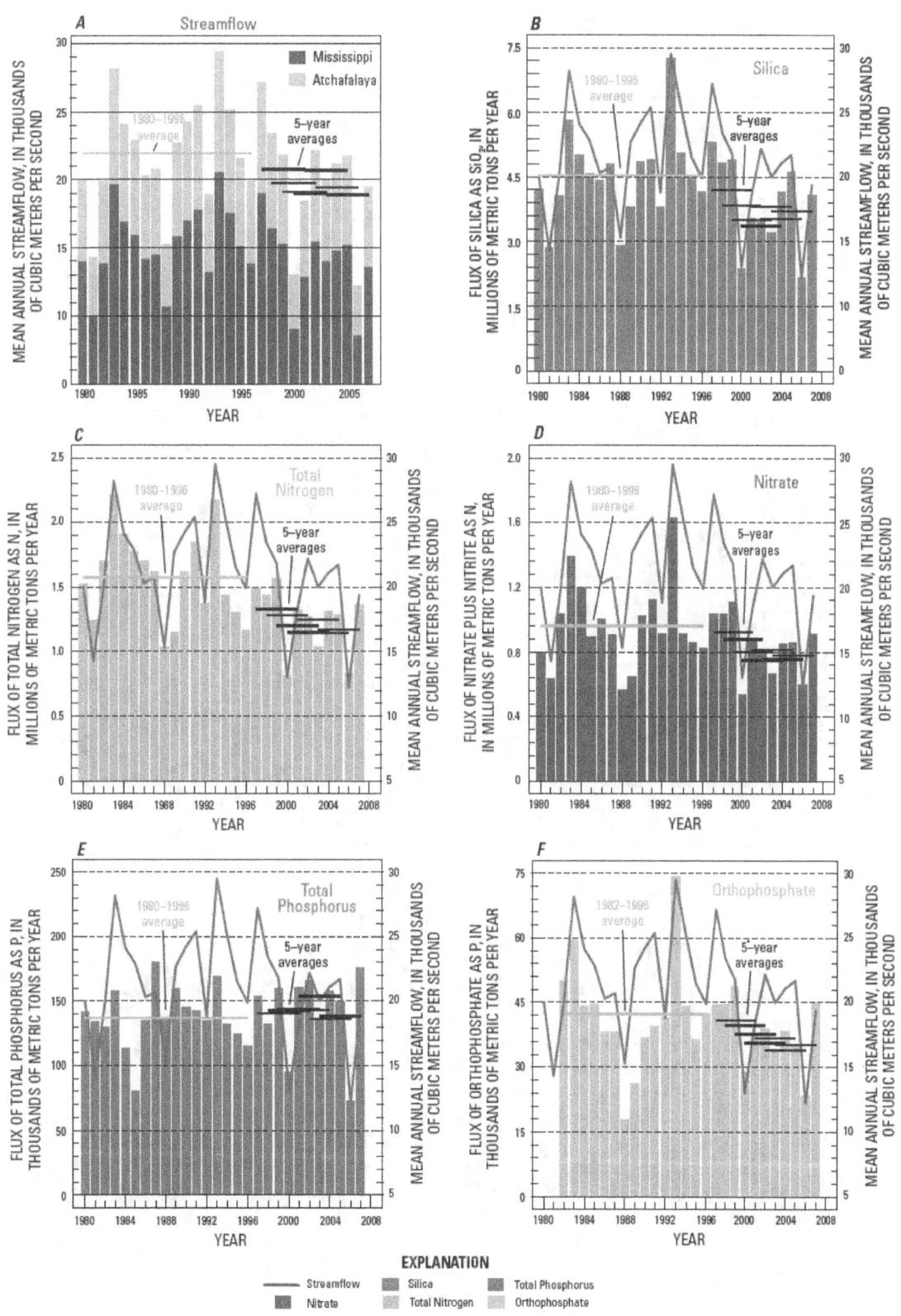

Figure 3. Mean annual (A) streamflow, and flux of (B) silica, (C) total nitrogen, (D) nitrate, (E) total phosphorus, and (F) orthophosphate, from the Mississippi-Atchafalaya River Basin to the Gulf of Mexico, 1980–2007.

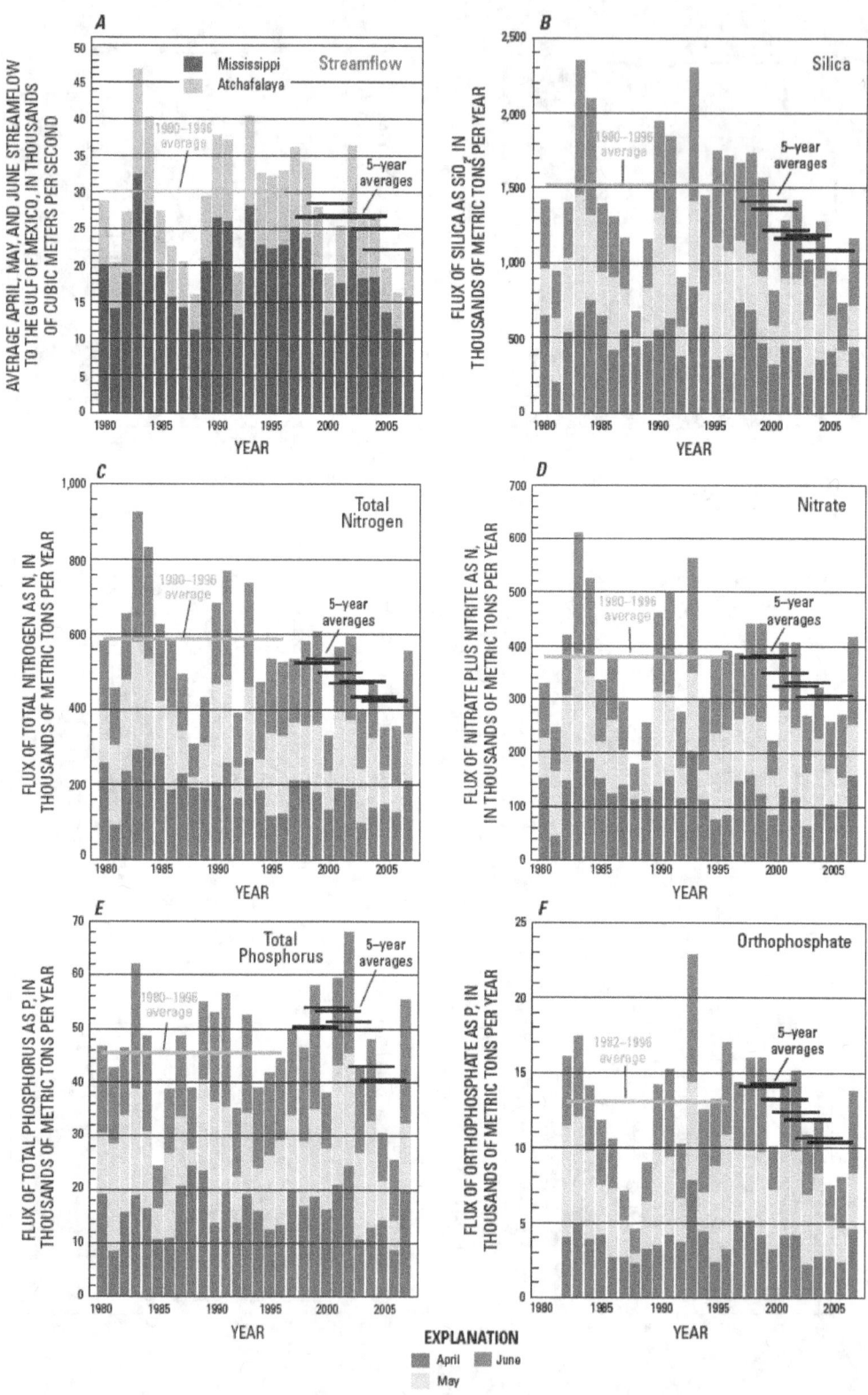

Figure 4.   Mean spring (April, May, and June) (A) streamflow, and flux of (B) silica, (C) total nitrogen, (D) nitrate, (E) total phosphorus, and (F) orthophosphate, from the Mississippi-Atchafalaya River Basin to the Gulf of Mexico, 1980–2007.

Table 4. Estimated mean annual fluxes of nutrients from the Mississippi-Atchafalaya River Basin to the Gulf of Mexico, 1980–1996, 2000–2004, 2001–2005, 2002–2006, and 2003–2007 calculated using LOADEST. [NA, not applicable; ammonium is part of total Kjeldahl nitrogen, so percentages of nitrogen components add to more than 100]

Nutrient	Mean flux (metric tons per year)	Percentage of total nitrogen or phosphorus flux
Silica as SiO2, dissolved—1980–1996	4,531,200	NA
Silica as SiO2, dissolved—2000–2004	3,366,000	NA
Silica as SiO2, dissolved—2001–2005	3,814,000	NA
Silica as SiO2, dissolved—2002–2006	3,534,000	NA
Silica as SiO2, dissolved—2003–2007	3,714,000	NA
Nitrogen (N), Total—1980–1996	1,575,200	100
Nitrogen (N), Total—2000–2004	1,148,000	100
Nitrogen (N), Total—2001–2005	1,242,800	100
Nitrogen (N), Total—2002–2006	1,146,200	100
Nitrogen (N), Total—2003–2007	1,166,400	100
Nitrate plus nitrite as N—1980–1996	961,500	61
Nitrate plus nitrite as N—2000–2004	749,400	65
Nitrate plus nitrite as N—2001–2005	813,400	65
Nitrate plus nitrite as N—2002–2006	757,000	66
Nitrate plus nitrite as N—2003–2007	779,000	67
Total Kjeldahl nitrogen as N—1980–1996	613,700	39
Total Kjeldahl nitrogen as N—2000–2004	398,600	35
Total Kjeldahl nitrogen as N—2001–2005	429,400	35
Total Kjeldahl nitrogen as N—2002–2006	389,200	34
Total Kjeldahl nitrogen as N—2003–2007	387,400	33
Ammonium as N—1980–1996	42,360	2.7
Ammonium as N—2000–2004	12,220	1.1
Ammonium as N—2001–2005	11,730	0.9
Ammonium as N—2002–2006	9,090	0.8
Ammonium as N—2003–2007	7,830	0.7
Phosphorus (P), Total—1980–1996	137,300	100
Phosphorus (P), Total—2000–2004	143,100	100
Phosphorus (P), Total—2001–2005	154,000	100
Phosphorus (P), Total—2002–2006	136,400	100
Phosphorus (P), Total—2003–2007	138,400	100
Orthophosphate as P—1982–1996	42,290	31
Orthophosphate as P—2000–2004	35,700	25
Orthophosphate as P—2001–2005	36,880	24
Orthophosphate as P—2002–2006	34,080	25
Orthophosphate as P—2003–2007	35,280	25

Table 5.   Mean monthly spring (April, May, June) flux of selected nutrients from the Mississippi-Atchafalaya River Basin to the Gulf of Mexico, 1980–1996, 2000–2004, 2001–2005, 2002–2006, and 2003–2007, calculated using LOADEST. [NA, not applicable; ammonium is part of total Kjeldahl nitrogen, so percentages of nitrogen components add to more than 100]

Nutrient	Mean flux (metric tons per month)	Percentage of total nitrogen or phosphorus flux
Silica as SiO2, dissolved – 1980–1996	506,300	NA
Silica as SiO2, dissolved – 2000–2004	387,700	NA
Silica as SiO2, dissolved – 2001–2005	396,100	NA
Silica as SiO2, dissolved – 2002–2006	359,500	NA
Silica as SiO2, dissolved – 2003–2007	342,900	NA
Nitrogen (N), Total – 1980–1996	196,100	100
Nitrogen (N), Total – 2000–2004	156,900	100
Nitrogen (N), Total – 2001–2005	158,400	100
Nitrogen (N), Total – 2002–2006	144,300	100
Nitrogen (N), Total – 2003–2007	141,800	100
Nitrate plus nitrite as N – 1980–1996	126,400	64
Nitrate plus nitrite as N – 2000–2004	108,300	69
Nitrate plus nitrite as N – 2001–2005	110,700	70
Nitrate plus nitrite as N – 2002–2006	101,700	71
Nitrate plus nitrite as N – 2003–2007	102,500	72
Total Kjeldahl nitrogen as N – 1980–1996	69,740	36
Total Kjeldahl nitrogen as N – 2000–2004	48,650	31
Total Kjeldahl nitrogen as N – 2001–2005	47,750	30
Total Kjeldahl nitrogen as N – 2002–2006	42,540	29
Total Kjeldahl nitrogen as N – 2003–2007	39,290	28
Ammonium as N – 1980–1996	4,790	2.4
Ammonium as N – 2000–2004	1,040	0.7
Ammonium as N – 2001–2005	900	0.5
Ammonium as N – 2002–2006	700	0.5
Ammonium as N – 2003–2007	470	0.3
Phosphorus (P), Total – 1980–1996	15,180	100
Phosphorus (P), Total – 2000–2004	17,110	100
Phosphorus (P), Total – 2001–2005	16,620	100
Phosphorus (P), Total – 2002–2006	14,350	100
Phosphorus (P), Total – 2003–2007	13,510	100
Orthophosphate as P – 1982–1996	4,350	29
Orthophosphate as P – 2000–2004	4,130	24
Orthophosphate as P – 2001–2005	3,960	24
Orthophosphate as P – 2002–2006	3,560	25
Orthophosphate as P – 2003–2007	3,470	26

The estimated mean spring nitrate flux from the MARB to the Gulf of Mexico for the 1980–1996 baseline period was 379,200 t (126,400 t per month) (table 5); hence, on average, approximately 39 percent of the nitrate flux occurred during these 3 months. The 5-year average mean spring nitrate flux for 2002–2006 was 305,100 t (101,700 t per month), a 20-percent decrease from the baseline period average. The 5-year average mean spring nitrate flux for 2003–2007 was 307,500 t (102,500 t per month), a 19-percent decrease from the baseline period average. Six of seven 5-year average mean spring nitrate fluxes for 1997–2007 were less than the mean spring nitrate flux for the baseline period and all seven were on average less by 10 percent (fig. 4). The spring flux of nitrate as a percentage of the TN flux increased from 64 percent during the baseline period to 72 percent during the 2003–2007 5-year period (table 5). Median spring nitrate flux for at least one of the seven 5-year periods was marginally significantly different (p=0.09) from the median spring nitrate flux for the baseline period.

Ammonium

The estimated mean annual flux of ammonium as N (ammonium) from the MARB to the Gulf of Mexico for the 1980–1996 baseline period is 42,360 t (table 4). The 5-year average mean annual ammonium flux for 2001–2005 was 11,730 t, a 72-percent decrease from the baseline period average. The 5-year average mean annual ammonium flux for 2002–2006 was 9,090 t, a 79-percent decrease from the baseline period average. The 5-year average mean annual ammonium flux for 2003–2007 was 7,830 t, an 82-percent decrease from the baseline period average. The seven 5-year average mean annual ammonium fluxes for 1997–2007 were all less than the mean annual ammonium flux for the baseline period and were on average less by 69 percent. The annual flux of ammonium as a percentage of the TN flux decreased from 2.7 percent during the baseline period to 0.7 percent during the 2003–2007 5-year period (table 4).

The estimated mean spring ammonium flux from the MARB to the Gulf of Mexico for the 1980–1996 baseline period was 14,370 t (4,790 t per month) (table 5); hence, on average, approximately 34 percent of the ammonium flux occurred during these 3 months. The 5-year average mean spring ammonium flux for 2002–2006 was 2,100 t (700 t per month), an 85-percent decrease from the baseline period average. The 5-year average mean spring ammonium flux for 2003–2007 was 1,410 t (470 t per month), a 90-percent decrease from the baseline period average. All seven 5-year average mean spring ammonium fluxes for 1997–2006 were less than the mean spring ammonium flux for the baseline period and were on average less by 76 percent. The spring flux of ammonium as a percentage of the TN flux decreased from 2.4 percent during the baseline period to 0.3 percent during the 2003–2007 5-year period.

Total Phosphorus

The estimated mean annual flux of total phosphorus as P (TP) from the MARB to the Gulf of Mexico for the 1980–1996 baseline period is 137,300 t (table 4). The 5-year average mean annual TP flux for 2001–2005 was 154,000 t, a 12-percent increase from the baseline period average. The 5-year average mean annual TP flux for 2002–2006 was 136,400 t, a 0.7-percent decrease from the baseline period average. The 5-year average mean annual TP flux for 2003–2007 was 138,420 t, a 12-percent increase from the baseline period average. Six of the seven 5-year average mean annual TP fluxes for 1997–2007 were greater than the mean annual TP flux for the baseline period and all seven were on average more by 4 percent (fig. 3). Median annual TP fluxes for the seven 5-year periods were not significantly different (p=0.73) from the median TP flux for the baseline period.

The estimated mean spring TP flux from the MARB to the Gulf of Mexico for the 1980–1996 baseline period was 45,540 t (15,180 t per month) (table 5); hence, on average, approximately 33 percent of the TP flux occurred during these 3 months. The 5-year average mean spring TP flux for 2002–2006 was 43,050 t (14,350 t per month), a 5.5-percent decrease from the baseline period average. The 5-year average mean spring TP flux for 2003–2007 was 40,530 t (13,510 t per month), an 11-percent decrease from the baseline period average. Five of the seven 5-year average mean spring TP fluxes for 1997–2006 were greater than the mean spring TP flux for the baseline period and all seven were on average more by 7.5 percent (fig. 4). Median spring TP flux for at least one of the seven 5-year periods was significantly different (p=0.05) from the median spring TP flux for the baseline period.

Orthophosphate

The estimated mean annual flux of orthophosphate as P (OP) from the MARB to the Gulf of Mexico for the 1982–1996 baseline period is 42,290 t (table 4). The 5-year average mean annual OP flux for 2001–2005 was 36,880 t, a 13-percent decrease from the baseline period average. The 5-year average mean annual OP flux for 2002–2006 was 34,080 t, a 19-percent decrease from the baseline period average. The 5-year average mean annual OP flux for 2003–2007 was 35,280 t, a 17-percent decrease from the baseline period average. All of the seven 5-year average mean annual OP fluxes for 1997–2007 were less than the mean annual OP flux for the baseline period and were on average less by 12 percent (fig. 3). The annual flux of OP as a percentage of the TP flux decreased from 31 percent during the baseline period to 25 percent during the 2003–2007 5-year period. Median annual OP flux for the seven 5-year periods was not significantly different (p=0.39) from the median OP fluxes for the baseline period.

The estimated mean spring OP flux from the MARB to the Gulf of Mexico for the 1982–1996 baseline period was 13,050 t (4,350 t per month) (table 5); hence, on average, approximately 31 percent of the OP flux occurred during these 3 months. The 5-year average mean spring OP flux for 2002–2006 was 10,680 t (3,560 t per month), an 18-percent decrease from the baseline period average. The 5-year average mean spring OP flux for 2003–2007 was 10,410 t (3,470 t per month), a 20-percent decrease from the baseline period average. Four of the seven 5-year average mean spring OP fluxes for 1997–2007 were less than the mean spring OP flux for the baseline period and all seven were on average less by 5 percent (fig. 4). The spring flux of OP as a percentage of the TP flux decreased from 29 percent during the baseline period to 26 percent during the 2003–2007 5-year period. Median spring OP flux for at least one of the seven 5-year periods was significantly different (p=0.04) from the median spring OP flux for the baseline period.

Nutrient Inputs

Estimates of mean annual inputs of N and P from fertilizer, manure, municipal and industrial point sources, and atmospheric deposition (N only) to the MARB are shown in figure 5. The mean annual input of N from fertilizer (both agricultural and nonagricultural) for the 1980–1996 baseline period was 6,227,800 t (table 6) or 56 percent of the total N inputs (sum of fertilizer, manure, atmospheric deposition,

and point sources) to the MARB (fig. 5). The 5-year average annual N input from fertilizer for 2000–2004 was 6,899,400 t, an 11-percent increase from the baseline period average, and 60 percent of the total N inputs to the MARB. The four 5-year average N inputs from fertilizer for 1997–2004 were all greater than the mean annual N input from fertilizer for the baseline period and were on average more by 12 percent (fig. 5). The mean annual input of P from fertilizer for the 1980–1996 baseline period was 1,049,500 t (table 7) or 50 percent of the total P inputs (sum of fertilizer, manure, and point sources) to the MARB (fig. 5). The 5-year average annual P input from fertilizer for 2000–2004 was 1,079,000 t, a 3-percent increase from the baseline period average, and 51 percent of the total P inputs to the MARB. The four 5-year average P inputs from fertilizer for 1997–2004 were all greater than the mean annual P input from fertilizer for the baseline period and were on average more by 2 percent (fig. 5).

The mean annual input of N from atmospheric deposition for the 1985–1996 baseline period was 1,207,200 t (table 6), or 11 percent of the total N inputs to the MARB. The estimates of N from atmospheric deposition reported here are not directly comparable with the atmospheric inputs of N reported by Goolsby and others (1999). The 5-year average N input from atmospheric deposition for 2000–2004 was 1,286,500 t, a 7-percent increase from the baseline period average, and 11 percent of the total N inputs to the MARB. The four 5-year average N inputs from atmospheric deposition for 1997–2004 were all greater than the mean annual N input from atmospheric deposition for the baseline period and were on average more by 6 percent (fig. 5).

Estimates of N and P inputs from manure are only available every 5 years, coincident with the release of Census of Agriculture data (U.S Department of Agriculture, 2008). Hence, the average of estimated inputs from 1982, 1987, and 1992 were used as the baseline input, and these were compared to the average of input estimates from 1997 and 2002. The mean annual input of N from manure for the baseline period was 3,303,100 t (table 6), or 30 percent of the total N inputs to the MARB. The average inputs of N from manure for 1997–2002 was 3,303,400 t, which is less than 0.1 percent less than the baseline period average, and 29 percent of the total N inputs to the MARB. The mean annual input of P from manure for the baseline period was 1,000,100 t (table 7), or 47 percent of the total P inputs to the MARB. The average inputs of P from manure for 1997–2002 was 998,600 t, which is 0.1 percent greater than the estimated annual input for the baseline period, and 47 percent of the total P inputs to the MARB (table 7).

Estimates of N and P inputs from municipal and industrial sources are only available for 1980, 1996, and 2004. Point-source inputs of N and P within the MARB based on 1996 permit information were estimated at 286,400 t/yr of N and 59,000 t/yr of P (Goolsby and others, 1999), both 3 percent of the total inputs to the MARB. An assessment of point sources within the MARB based on 2004 permit information estimated N inputs at 233,000 t/yr and P inputs at 39,500 t/yr

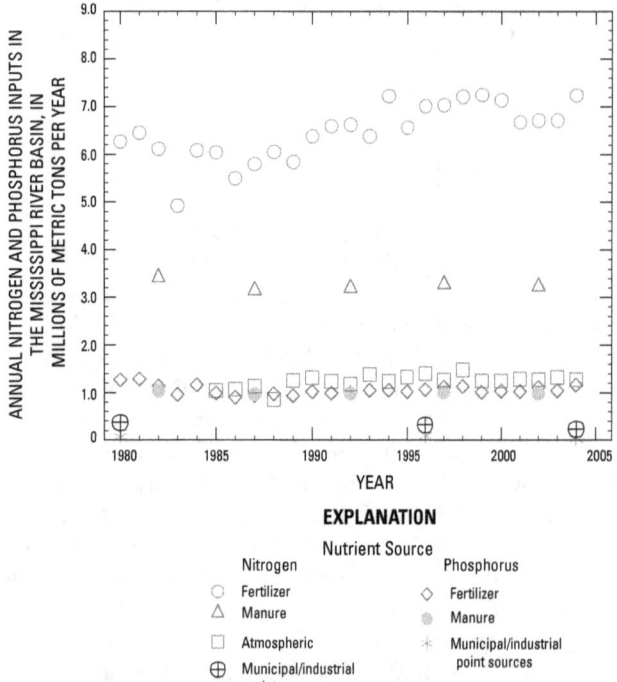

Figure 5. Annual inputs to the Mississippi-Atchafalaya River Basin, 1980–2004, of nitrogen from fertilizer, manure, municipal and industrial point sources, and the atmosphere; and phosphorus from fertilizer, manure, and municipal and industrial point sources.

Table 6. Mean annual nitrogen inputs to the entire Mississippi-Atchafalaya River Basin and to 10 large subbasins in the Mississippi-Atchafalaya River Basin, 1980–1996 and 2000–2004. [NC, not calculated; t, metric tons]

Site name and subbasin number(s)	Mean annual N input from fertilizer (t)		Mean annual N input from manure (t)		Mean annual N input from atmospheric deposition (t)	
	1980–1996	2000–2004	1982–1996	1997–2002	1985–1996	2000–2004
Mississippi River at Clinton, Iowa (1)	559,100	604,500	349,500	300,200	106,400	121,300
Mississippi River below Grafton, Ill. (1,2)	1,845,600	1,876,900	714,300	603,600	232,600	246,600
Missouri River at Omaha, Nebr. (3)	593,500	945,900	542,500	535,800	152,800	180,700
Missouri River at Hermann, Mo. (3,4)	1,848,500	2,306,700	1,196,100	1,193,400	346,100	391,200
Mississippi River at Thebes, Ill. (1,2,3,4,5)	3,848,800	4,328,200	1,952,800	1,834,100	602,800	662,200
Ohio River at Cannelton Dam at Cannelton, Ind. (6)	344,700	360,700	213,700	190,800	144,800	140,900
Ohio River at Dam 53 near Grand Chain, Ill. (6,7)	1,092,600	1,100,700	522,700	503,700	285,800	285,700
Arkansas River below Little Rock, Ark. (8)	571,200	659,700	451,500	527,200	139,700	147,800
Red River at Alexandria, La. (9)	287,000	307,700	246,300	299,800	95,200	101,500
Mississippi River near St. Francisville, La. (1,2,3,4,5,6,7,8,10)	5,940,800	6,591,700	3,056,800	3,003,600	1,112,000	1,185,000
Atchafalaya River at Melville, La. (9,11)	NC	NC	NC	NC	NC	NC
Entire Mississippi-Atchafalaya River Basin (1–11)	6,227,800	6,899,400	3,303,100	3,303,400	1,207,200	1,286,500

Table 7. Mean annual phosphorus inputs to the entire Mississippi-Atchafalaya River Basin and to 10 large subbasins in the Mississippi-Atchafalaya River Basin, 1980–1996 and 2000–2004. [NC, not calculated; t, metric tons]

Site name and subbasin number(s)	Mean annual P input from fertilizer (t)		Mean annual P input from manure (t)	
	1980–1996	2000–2004	1982–1996	1997–2002
Mississippi River at Clinton, Iowa (1)	105,300	101,900	90,500	82,990
Mississippi River below Grafton, Ill. (1,2)	334,000	301,900	212,300	187,300
Missouri River at Omaha, Nebr. (3)	106,100	163,400	168,600	167,700
Missouri River at Hermann, Mo. (3,4)	256,500	355,400	370,500	365,000
Mississippi River at Thebes, Ill. (1,2,3,4,5)	619,900	681,300	596,400	564,100
Ohio River at Cannelton Dam at Cannelton, Ind. (6)	80,720	67,880	213,700	190,800
Ohio River at Dam 53 near Grand Chain, Ill. (6,7)	247,900	203,900	156,800	151,400
Arkansas River below Little Rock, Ark. (8)	72,470	81,510	13,420	15,440
Red River at Alexandria, La. (9)	38,230	35,210	73,210	86,850
Mississippi River near St. Francisville, La. (1,2,3,4,5,6,7,8,10)	1,011,300	1,043,700	926,900	911,700
Atchafalaya River at Melville, La. (9,11)	NC	NC	NC	NC
Entire Mississippi-Atchafalaya River basin (1–11)	1,049,500	1,079,000	1,000,100	998,600

(Mississippi River/Gulf of Mexico Watershed Nutrient Task Force, 2006; U.S. Environmental Protection Agency, 2007), both 2 percent of the total inputs to the MARB. Hence, there was a decrease in point-source inputs of both N and P between the baseline period and the recent period.

Eleven Sites on the Mississippi and Atchafalaya Rivers and Their Major Tributaries

Eleven sites (table 1) are used to determine the streamflow and nutrient flux feom 11 major subbasins of the MARB. The drainage areas of these basins range from 175,000 to 2,967,000 square kilometers. Most of the sites are on the main stem of the Mississippi River or are near to the mouths of major tributaries to the Mississippi River (fig. 1).

Streamflow

The estimated mean annual streamflows from the 11 major subbasins in the MARB for the 1980–1996 baseline period and the 2000–2004, 2001–2005, and 2002–2006 5-year average periods are given in table 8. The 2001–2005 5-year average mean annual streamflows were less than or equal to the baseline mean annual streamflows at 9 of 11 sites, with the decreases ranging from 0 to 31 percent. The Ohio River at Cannelton Dam, Ind., and the Ohio River at Dam 53 near Grand Chain, Ill., had increased streamflows of 17 and 6 percent, respectively (table 8). The 2002–2006 5-year average mean annual streamflows were less than the baseline mean annual streamflows at 9 of 11 sites, with the decreases ranging from 10 to 40 percent. The Ohio River at Cannelton Dam, Ind., and the Ohio River at Dam 53 near Grand Chain, Ill., had increased streamflows of 19 and 7 percent, respectively (table 8).

The estimated mean spring streamflows from the 11 major subbasins in MARB for the 1980–1996 baseline period and the 2000–2004, 2001–2005, and 2002–2006 5-year averages are given in table 9. The 2001–2005 5-year average mean spring streamflows were less than the baseline mean spring streamflows at 8 of 11 sites, with the decreases ranging from 0.3 to 35 percent. Three sites had increased mean spring streamflow: the Ohio River at Cannelton Dam, Ind. (20 percent); the Mississippi River at Clinton, Iowa (18 percent); and the Mississippi River below Grafton, Ill. (8 percent) (table 9). The 2002–2006 5-year average mean spring streamflows were less than the baseline mean spring streamflows at 8 of 11 sites, with the decreases ranging from 7 to 44 percent. Three sites had increased mean spring streamflow: the Ohio River at Cannelton Dam, Ind. (19 percent); the Mississippi River at Clinton, Iowa (1 percent); and the Ohio River at Dam 53 near Grand Chain, Ill. (1 percent).

Silica

The estimated mean annual silica flux from 11 major subbasins in MARB for the 1980–1996 baseline period and the 2000–2004, 2001–2005, and 2002–2006 5-year averages are given in table 10. Estimates of the lower and upper 95-percent confidence values for nutrient flux estimates from the 11 subbasins are not provided here, but are in Aulenbach and others (2007). Silica flux was not available for the more recent 5-year averages for the Red River at Alexandria, La.; hence, comparisons of the 5-year averages were made only for the remaining 10 sites. The 2001–2005 5-year average mean annual silica fluxes were less than the baseline mean annual silica fluxes at 9 of 10 sites, with the decreases ranging from 0.4 to 40 percent. Only the Ohio River at Dam 53 near Grand Chain, Ill. (8 percent) had increased silica flux. The

Table 8.   Mean annual streamflow from 11 sites on the Mississippi River and its major tributaries, 1980–1996, 2000–2004, 2001–2005, and 2002–2006. [(m³/s), cubic meters per second]

Site name	Mean annual streamflow, (m³/s)			
	1980–1996	2000–2004	2001–2005	2002–2006
Mississippi River at Clinton, Iowa	1,590	1,530	1,530	1,430
Mississippi River below Grafton, Ill.	3,680	3,060	3,180	2,840
Missouri River at Omaha, Nebr.	1,010	830	760	720
Missouri River at Hermann, Mo.	2,760	1,820	1,900	1,660
Mississippi River at Thebes, Ill.	6,870	5,310	5,590	5,040
Ohio River at Cannelton Dam at Cannelton, Ind.	3,620	3,910	4,230	4,310
Ohio River at Dam 53 near Grand Chain, Ill.	8,400	8,010	8,870	8,980
Arkansas River below Little Rock, Ark.	1,420	1,000	1,080	900
Red River at Alexandria, La.	1,050	990	1,050	850
Mississippi River near St. Francisville, La.	15,350	13,260	14,480	13,610
Atchafalaya River at Melville, La.	6,590	5,680	6,200	5,830

Table 9. Spring (April, May, June) mean monthly streamflow from 11 sites on the Mississippi River and its major tributaries, 1980–1996, 2000–2004, 2001–2005, and 2002–2006. [(m³/s), cubic meters per second]

Site name	Spring mean monthly streamflow, (m³/s)			
	1980–1996	2000–2004	2001–2005	2002–2006
Mississippi River at Clinton, Iowa	2,390	2,760	2,830	2,410
Mississippi River below Grafton, Ill.	5,240	5,550	5,640	4,860
Missouri River at Omaha, Nebr.	1,210	1,000	970	890
Missouri River at Hermann, Mo.	3,850	2,720	2,880	2,370
Mississippi River at Thebes, Ill.	9,720	8,880	9,100	7,910
Ohio River at Cannelton Dam at Cannelton, Ind.	4,610	5,480	5,540	5,490
Ohio River at Dam 53 near Grand Chain, Ill.	10,190	10,050	10,160	10,260
Arkansas River below Little Rock, Ark.	2,240	1,560	1,450	1,340
Red River at Alexandria, La.	1,480	1,150	1,000	830
Mississippi River near St. Francisville, La.	21,040	18,680	18,780	17,510
Atchafalaya River at Melville, La.	9,060	7,990	8,030	7,500

Table 10. Mean annual silica flux from 11 sites on the Mississippi River and its major tributaries, 1980–1996, 2000–2004, 2001–2005, and 2002–2006. [ND, not determined because one-half or more of the annual flux estimates are missing; t, metric tons]

Site name	Mean annual flux of silica as SiO_2, (t)			
	1980–1996	2000–2004	2001–2005	2002–2006
Mississippi River at Clinton, Iowa	589,750	463,200	468,800	368,200
Mississippi River below Grafton, Ill.	1,042,900	752,200	816,000	656,000
Missouri River at Omaha, Nebr.	316,630	225,400	218,400	167,200
Missouri River at Hermann, Mo.	872,760	540,000	562,200	484,400
Mississippi River at Thebes, Ill.	2,056,500	1,286,200	1,396,200	1,189,600
Ohio River at Cannelton Dam at Cannelton, Ind.	761,750	690,400	759,000	766,200
Ohio River at Dam 53 near Grand Chain, Ill.	1,330,500	1,239,400	1,442,400	1,498,000
Arkansas River below Little Rock, Ark.	362,890	198,600	218,200	174,320
Red River at Alexandria, La.	243,230	ND	ND	ND
Mississippi River near St. Francisville, La.	3,171,800	2,390,000	2,708,000	2,494,000
Atchafalaya River at Melville, La.	1,359,000	977,000	1,106,200	1,038,600

2002–2006 5-year average mean annual silica fluxes were less than the baseline mean annual silica fluxes at 8 of 10 sites, with the decreases ranging from 21 to 52 percent. Only the Ohio River at Dam 53 near Grand Chain, Ill. (13 percent) and the Ohio River at Cannelton Dam, Ind. (1 percent) had increased silica flux (table 10).

The estimated mean spring silica flux from 10 major subbasins in MARB for the 1980–1996 baseline period and the 2000–2004, 2001–2005, and 2002–2006 5-year averages are given in table 11. The 2001–2005 5-year average mean spring silica fluxes were less than or equal to the baseline mean spring silica flux at 8 of 10 sites, with the decreases ranging from 5 to 56 percent. Two sites had increased mean spring silica flux: the Mississippi River at Clinton, Iowa (2-percent increase) and the Mississippi River below Grafton, Ill. (22-percent increase). The 2002–2006 5-year average mean spring silica fluxes were less than or equal to the baseline mean spring silica flux at all 10 sites, with the decreases ranging from 2 to 59 percent (table 11).

Total Nitrogen

The estimated mean annual total nitrogen as N (TN) flux from 11 major subbasins in MARB for the 1980–1996 baseline period and the 2000–2004, 2001–2005, and 2002–2006 5-year averages are given in table 12. The 2001–2005 5-year average mean annual TN fluxes were less than the baseline mean annual TN fluxes at all 11 sites, with the decreases ranging from 2 to 54 percent. The 2002–2006 5-year average mean annual TN fluxes were less than the baseline mean annual TN fluxes at all 11 sites, with the decreases ranging from 1 to 55 percent (table 12).

The estimated mean spring TN flux from 11 major subbasins in MARB for the 1980–1996 baseline period and the 2000–2004, 2001–2005, and 2002–2006 5-year averages are given in table 13. The 2001–2005 5-year average mean spring TN fluxes were less than the baseline mean annual TN fluxes at 9 of 11 sites, with the decreases ranging from 1 to 57 percent. The Mississippi River at Clinton, Iowa (44 percent) and the Mississippi River below Grafton, Ill. (16 percent) had increases in spring TN flux. The 2002–2006 5-year average mean spring TN fluxes were less than the baseline mean annual TN fluxes at 10 of 11 sites, with the decreases ranging from 0.1 to 64 percent. Only the Mississippi River at Clinton, Iowa had an increase (35 percent) in spring TN flux (table 13).

Nitrate

The estimated mean annual total nitrate plus nitrite as N (nitrate) flux from 11 major subbasins in MARB for the 1980–1996 baseline period and the 2000–2004, 2001–2005, and 2002–2006 5-year averages are given in table 14. The 2001–2005 5-year average mean annual nitrate fluxes were less than the baseline mean annual nitrate fluxes at 9 of 11 sites, with the decreases ranging from 1 to 55 percent. The two sites had increases in nitrate flux: the Mississippi River at Clinton, Iowa (14 percent) and the Ohio River at Cannelton Dam, Ind. (5 percent). The 2002–2006 5-year average mean annual nitrate fluxes were less than the baseline mean annual nitrate fluxes at 8 of 11 sites, with the decreases ranging from 18 to 53 percent. The Mississippi River at Clinton, Iowa (22 percent), the Ohio River at Cannelton Dam, Ind. (4 percent), and the Ohio River at Dam 53 near Grand Chain, Ill. (1 percent) had increased nitrate flux (table 14).

Table 11. Spring (April, May, June) mean monthly silica flux from 11 sites on the Mississippi River and its major tributaries, 1980–1996, 2000–2004, 2001–2005, and 2002–2006. [ND, not determined because one-half or more of the spring-flux estimates are missing; t, metric tons]

Site name	Spring mean monthly flux of silica as SiO_2 (t)			
	1980–1996	2000–2004	2001–2005	2002–2006
Mississippi River at Clinton, Iowa	62,520	73,890	75,620	44,430
Mississippi River below Grafton, Ill.	106,480	129,710	130,170	97,550
Missouri River at Omaha, Nebr.	32,570	23,000	23,233	21,450
Missouri River at Hermann, Mo.	100,880	65,860	70,210	56,690
Mississippi River at Thebes, Ill.	228,810	184,580	188,930	151,290
Ohio River at Cannelton Dam at Cannelton, Ind.	89,720	82,160	79,590	75,790
Ohio River at Dam 53 near Grand Chain, Ill.	124,630	116,860	118,800	122,600
Arkansas River below Little Rock, Ark.	48,720	23,180	21,530	19,950
Red River at Alexandria, La.	23,060	ND	ND	ND
Mississippi River near St. Francisville, La.	355,510	278,930	284,730	255,130
Atchafalaya River at Melville, La.	150,780	108,610	111,470	104,370

Table 12. Mean annual total nitrogen flux from 11 sites on the Mississippi River and its major tributaries, 1980–1996, 2000–2004, 2001–2005, and 2002–2006. [TN, total nitrogen; t, metric tons]

Site name	Mean annual flux of TN as nitrogen, (t)			
	1980–1996	2000–2004	2001–2005	2002–2006
Mississippi River at Clinton, Iowa	145,040	129,820	138,360	142,820
Mississippi River below Grafton, Ill.	539,310	411,680	447,160	392,140
Missouri River at Omaha, Nebr.	106,780	46,860	49,460	47,760
Missouri River at Hermann, Mo.	251,770	145,760	162,380	130,280
Mississippi River at Thebes, Ill.	866,470	597,200	647,200	556,400
Ohio River at Cannelton Dam at Cannelton, Ind.	266,980	239,620	252,080	251,840
Ohio River at Dam 53 near Grand Chain, Ill.	518,480	469,020	509,600	515,600
Arkansas River below Little Rock, Ark.	54,870	37,010	41,470	34,700
Red River at Alexandria, La.	37,640	28,290	31,050	24,400
Mississippi River near St. Francisville, La.	1,180,000	853,400	922,800	842,800
Atchafalaya River at Melville, La.	395,120	295,040	330,600	303,740

Table 13. Spring (April, May, June) mean monthly total nitrogen flux from 11 sites on the Mississippi River and its major tributaries, 1980–1996, 2000–2004, 2001–2005, and 2002–2006. [TN, total nitrogen; t, metric tons]

Site name	Spring mean monthly flux of TN as nitrogen, (t)			
	1980–1996	2000–2004	2001–2005	2002–2006
Mississippi River at Clinton, Iowa	18,180	23,540	26,190	24,460
Mississippi River below Grafton, Ill.	67,630	74,600	78,200	67,570
Missouri River at Omaha, Nebr.	14,270	7,040	7,810	7,080
Missouri River at Hermann, Mo.	38,030	24,940	27,300	20,840
Mississippi River at Thebes, Ill.	119,530	104,010	108,270	90,300
Ohio River at Cannelton Dam at Cannelton, Ind.	28,910	26,570	26,570	25,700
Ohio River at Dam 53 near Grand Chain, Ill.	55,010	54,970	54,360	54,490
Arkansas River below Little Rock, Ark.	7,420	4,610	4,360	4,130
Red River at Alexandria, La.	4,590	2,310	1,990	1,640
Mississippi River near St. Francisville, La.	147,680	116,540	117,430	105,440
Atchafalaya River at Melville, La.	48,430	40,390	41,000	38,860

Table 14. Mean annual nitrate plus nitrite flux from 11 sites on the Mississippi River and its major tributaries, 1980–1996, 2000–2004, 2001–2005, and 2002–2006. [t, metric tons]

Site name	Mean annual flux of nitrate plus nitrite as nitrogen, (t)			
	1980–1996	2000–2004	2001–2005	2002–2006
Mississippi River at Clinton, Iowa	77,530	81,720	88,260	94,860
Mississippi River below Grafton, Ill.	371,190	296,000	325,400	284,400
Missouri River at Omaha, Nebr.	53,340	21,040	24,060	25,280
Missouri River at Hermann, Mo.	131,770	70,060	78,620	66,660
Mississippi River at Thebes, Ill.	547,760	391,200	427,800	369,200
Ohio River at Cannelton Dam at Cannelton, Ind.	152,750	152,800	160,000	159,600
Ohio River at Dam 53 near Grand Chain, Ill.	338,120	308,800	334,800	340,800
Arkansas River below Little Rock, Ark.	24,780	17,850	21,930	18,830
Red River at Alexandria, La.	8,990	6,070	6,750	4,820
Mississippi River near St. Francisville, La.	737,100	574,600	623,400	572,400
Atchafalaya River at Melville, La.	224,410	174,800	190,000	184,600

Table 15.   Spring (April, May, June) mean monthly nitrate plus nitrite flux from 11 sites on the Mississippi River and its major tributaries, 1980–1996, 2000–2004, 2001–2005, and 2002–2006. [t, metric tons]

Site name	Spring mean monthly flux of nitrate plus nitrite as nitrogen, (t)			
	1980–1996	2000–2004	2001–2005	2002–2006
Mississippi River at Clinton, Iowa	9,620	15,400	17,630	16,860
Mississippi River below Grafton, Ill.	46,960	55,030	58,140	50,410
Missouri River at Omaha, Nebr.	7,870	3,350	3,940	3,990
Missouri River at Hermann, Mo.	20,410	11,910	13,390	10,990
Mississippi River at Thebes, Ill.	77,710	69,350	72,850	61,390
Ohio River at Cannelton Dam at Cannelton, Ind.	17,000	17,090	16,930	16,340
Ohio River at Dam 53 near Grand Chain, Ill.	36,430	37,680	37,070	37,210
Arkansas River below Little Rock, Ark.	3,230	2,160	2,190	2,150
Red River at Alexandria, La.	990	320	270	190
Mississippi River near St. Francisville, La.	97,210	82,750	84,370	76,130
Atchafalaya River at Melville, La.	29,140	25,540	26,310	25,630

The estimated mean spring nitrate flux from 11 major subbasins in MARB for the 1980–1996 baseline period and the 2000–2004, 2001–2005, and 2002–2006 5-year averages are given in table 15. The 2001–2005 5-year average mean spring nitrate fluxes were less than the baseline mean annual nitrate fluxes at 8 of 11 sites, with the decreases ranging from 0.4 to 73 percent. The Mississippi River at Clinton, Iowa (83 percent), the Mississippi River below Grafton, Ill. (24 percent), and the Ohio River at Dam 53 near Grand Chain, Ill. (2 percent) had increased spring nitrate flux. The 2002–2006 5-year average mean spring nitrate fluxes were less than the baseline annual nitrate fluxes at 8 of 11 sites, with the decreases ranging from 4 to 81 percent. The Mississippi River at Clinton, Iowa (75 percent), the Mississippi River below Grafton, Ill. (7 percent), and the Ohio River at Dam 53 near Grand Chain, Ill. (2 percent) had increased spring nitrate flux (table 15).

Total Phosphorus

The estimated mean annual total phosphorus as P (TP) flux from 11 major subbasins in MARB for the 1980–1996 baseline period and the 2000–2004, 2001–2005, and 2002–2006 5-year averages are given in table 16. The 2001–2005 5-year average mean annual TP fluxes were greater than the baseline mean annual TP fluxes at 7 of 11 sites, with the increases ranging from 6 to 51 percent. Five-year average mean annual TP fluxes were less than the baseline mean annual TP fluxes at 4 sites, with the decreases ranging from 4 to 46 percent. The 2002–2006 5-year average mean annual TP fluxes were less than or equal to the baseline mean annual TP fluxes at 9 of 11 sites, with the decreases ranging from 0 to 55 percent. Five-year average mean annual TP fluxes were greater than the baseline mean annual TP fluxes at the Ohio River at Dam 53 near Grand Chain, Ill. (52 percent) and the Ohio River at Cannelton Dam, Ind. (45 percent) (table 16).

The estimated mean spring TP flux from 11 major subbasins in MARB for the 1980–1996 baseline period and the 2000–2004, 2001–2005, and 2002–2006 5-year averages are given in table 17. The 2001–2005 5-year average mean spring TP fluxes were greater than the baseline mean spring TP fluxes at 8 of 11 sites, with the increases ranging from 8 to 60 percent. The three sites with decreases in spring TP flux were the Missouri River at Omaha, Nebr. (45 percent), the Arkansas River below Little Rock, Ark. (23 percent), and the Red River at Alexandria, La. (76 percent). The 2002–2006 5-year average mean spring TP fluxes were less than the baseline mean spring TP fluxes at 6 of 11 sites, with the decreases ranging from 5 to 80 percent. The mean spring TP fluxes were greater than the baseline mean spring TP fluxes at 5 of 11 sites, with the increases ranging from 8 to 45 percent (table 17).

Orthophosphate

The estimated mean annual orthophosphate as P (OP) flux from the 11 major subbasins in MARB for the 1982–1996 baseline period and the 2000–2004, 2001–2005, and 2002–2006 5-year averages are given in table 18. OP flux was not available for the baseline period for the Ohio River at Cannelton Dam, Ind.; hence, comparisons with more recent 5-year averages were made only for the remaining 10 sites. The 2001–2005 5-year average mean annual OP fluxes were less than the baseline mean annual OP fluxes at 9 of 10 sites, with the decreases ranging from 11 to 45 percent. The Red River at Alexandria, La., had increased (15 percent) mean annual OP flux. The 2002–2006 5-year average mean annual OP fluxes were less than the baseline mean annual OP fluxes at all 9 sites, with the decreases ranging from 16 to 49 percent. The comparison could not be made for the Ohio River at Cannelton Dam, Ind., and the Red River at Alexandria, La. (table 18).

The estimated mean spring OP flux from 11 major subbasins in MARB for the 1982–1996 baseline period and the

Table 16.   Mean annual total phosphorus flux from 11 sites on the Mississippi River and its major tributaries, 1980–1996, 2000–2004, 2001–2005, and 2002–2006. [TP, total phosphorus; t, metric tons]

Site name	Mean annual flux of TP as phosphorus, (t)			
	1980–1996	2000–2004	2001–2005	2002–2006
Mississippi River at Clinton, Iowa	9,260	8,520	8,460	7,680
Mississippi River below Grafton, Ill.	28,070	28,400	29,720	25,200
Missouri River at Omaha, Nebr.	14,980	8,420	8,120	6,810
Missouri River at Hermann, Mo.	27,710	27,800	30,420	21,700
Mississippi River at Thebes, Ill.	64,680	66,320	70,900	55,960
Ohio River at Cannelton Dam at Cannelton, Ind.	24,010	32,460	35,240	34,880
Ohio River at Dam 53 near Grand Chain, Ill.	38,840	52,600	58,720	59,020
Arkansas River below Little Rock, Ark.	4,590	4,150	4,420	3,610
Red River at Alexandria, La.	7,100	3,580	4,270	3,220
Mississippi River near St. Francisville, La.	97,560	102,560	110,060	97,100
Atchafalaya River at Melville, La.	39,720	40,940	44,500	39,720

Table 17.   Spring (April, May, June) mean monthly total phosphorus flux from 11 sites on the Mississippi River and its major tributaries, 1980–1996, 2000–2004, 2001–2005, and 2002–2006. [TP, total phosphorus; t, metric tons]

Site name	Spring mean monthly flux of TP as phosphorus, (t)			
	1980–1996	2000–2004	2001–2005	2002–2006
Mississippi River at Clinton, Iowa	1,160	1,490	1,510	1,250
Mississippi River below Grafton, Ill.	3,180	5,020	5,080	4,100
Missouri River at Omaha, Nebr.	2,470	1,320	1,370	1,050
Missouri River at Hermann, Mo.	3,860	4,980	5,360	3,540
Mississippi River at Thebes, Ill.	7,890	12,060	12,260	9,070
Ohio River at Cannelton Dam at Cannelton, Ind.	2,590	3,560	3,610	3,450
Ohio River at Dam 53 near Grand Chain, Ill.	3,740	5,370	5,320	5,410
Arkansas River below Little Rock, Ark.	620	520	480	450
Red River at Alexandria, La.	990	280	240	190
Mississippi River near St. Francisville, La.	10,480	12,000	11,560	9,900
Atchafalaya River at Melville, La.	4,690	5,110	5,060	4,450

Table 18.   Mean annual orthophosphate flux from 11 sites on the Mississippi River and its major tributaries, 1982–1996, 2000–2004, 2001–2005, and 2002–2006. [ND, not determined because one-half or more of the annual flux estimates are missing; OP, orthophosphate; t, metric tons]

Site name	Mean annual flux of OP as phosphorus, (t)			
	1982–1996	2000–2004	2001–2005	2002–2006
Mississippi River at Clinton, Iowa	4,150	3,430	3,700	3,430
Mississippi River below Grafton, Ill.	11,390	9,402	9,952	8,800
Missouri River at Omaha, Nebr.	1,690	890	934	860
Missouri River at Hermann, Mo.	7,260	4,510	4,830	4,240
Mississippi River at Thebes, Ill.	25,980	16,580	17,940	15,740
Ohio River at Cannelton Dam at Cannelton, Ind.	ND	5,520	5,500	5,130
Ohio River at Dam 53 near Grand Chain, Ill.	12,270	9,180	9,840	10,360
Arkansas River below Little Rock, Ark.	2,220	1,390	1,560	1,350
Red River at Alexandria, La.	2,610	2,540	3,000	ND
Mississippi River near St. Francisville, La.	30,990	26,200	27,100	24,760
Atchafalaya River at Melville, La.	11,310	9,500	9,790	9,320

Table 19. Spring (April, May, June) mean monthly orthophosphate flux from 11 sites on the Mississippi River and its major tributaries, 1982–1996, 2000–2004, 2001–2005, and 2002–2006. [ND, not determined because one-half or more of the spring flux estimates are missing; OP, orthophosphate; t, metric tons]

Site name	Spring mean monthly flux of OP as phosphorus, (t)			
	1982–1996	2000–2004	2001–2005	2002–2006
Mississippi River at Clinton, Iowa	480	400	440	330
Mississippi River below Grafton, Ill.	1,120	1,430	1,420	1,150
Missouri River at Omaha, Nebr.	240	120	130	100
Missouri River at Hermann, Mo.	840	590	640	540
Mississippi River at Thebes, Ill.	2,560	2,130	2,230	1,880
Ohio River at Cannelton Dam at Cannelton, Ind.	ND	500	450	410
Ohio River at Dam 53 near Grand Chain, Ill.	890	810	730	750
Arkansas River below Little Rock, Ark.	280	180	170	160
Red River at Alexandria, La.	360	190	180	ND
Mississippi River near St. Francisville, La.	3,090	3,010	2,880	2,540
Atchafalaya River at Melville, La.	1,260	1,230	1,080	970

2000–2004, 2001–2005, and 2002–2006 5-year averages are given in table 19. The 2001–2005 5-year average mean spring OP fluxes were less than the baseline mean spring OP fluxes at 9 of 10 sites, with the decreases ranging from 7 to 50 percent. The Mississippi River below Grafton, Ill. had increased (27 percent) mean spring OP flux. The 2002–2006 5-year average mean spring OP fluxes were less than the baseline mean spring OP fluxes at 8 of 9 sites, with the decreases ranging from 16 to 58 percent. The Mississippi River below Grafton, Ill. had increased (3 percent) mean spring OP flux, and the comparison could not be made at the Ohio River at Cannelton Dam, Ind., and the Red River at Alexandria, La. (table 19).

Nutrient Inputs

Estimates of mean annual inputs from fertilizer, manure, and atmospheric deposition (N only) to 10 major subbasins in MARB for the 1980–1996 baseline period and the 2000–2004 5-year period are given in tables 6 for N and 7 for P. Inputs are given for entire subbasins and not just the downstream portion of nested basins. Inputs are not given for the Atchafalaya River at Melville, La., subbasin. The 5-year mean annual N inputs from fertilizer for 2000–2004 were greater than the baseline period mean annual N inputs from fertilizer in all 10 subbasins, with the increases ranging from 1 percent for the Ohio River at Dam 53 near Grand Chain, Ill., to 60 percent for the Missouri River at Omaha, Nebr. (table 6). The mean annual N inputs from manure for 1997–2002 were less than the baseline period mean annual N inputs from manure in 8 of the 10 subbasins, with the decreases ranging from 0.2 per cent for the Missouri River at Hermann, Mo., to 15 percent for the Mississippi River below Grafton, Ill. Mean annual N inputs from manure for 1997–2002 were greater than the inputs for the baseline period for the Arkansas River below Little Rock, Ark. (17 percent), and the Red River at Alexandria, La. (22 percent) (table 6). The 5-year mean annual N inputs from

atmospheric deposition for 2000–2004 were greater than the baseline period mean annual N inputs from atmospheric deposition in 8 of the 10 subbasins, with the increases ranging from 6 percent for the Mississippi River below Grafton, Ill., to 18 percent for the Missouri River at Omaha, Nebr. The mean annual N inputs from atmospheric deposition for 2000–2004 were less than the mean annual N inputs for the baseline period for the Ohio River near Cannelton Dam, Ind. (3 percent), and the Ohio River near Grand Chain, Ill. (less than 1 percent) (table 6).

The 5-year mean annual P inputs from fertilizer for 2000–2004 were greater than the baseline period mean annual P input from fertilizer in 5 of the 10 subbasins, with the increases ranging from 3 to 54 percent for the Missouri River at Omaha, Nebr., and the decreases ranging from 3 percent for the Mississippi River at Clinton, Iowa, to 18 percent for the Ohio River near Grand Chain, Ill. (table 7). The mean annual P inputs from manure for 1997–2002 were less than the baseline period mean annual P inputs from manure in 8 of the 10 subbasins, with the decreases ranging from 0.5 percent for the Missouri River at Omaha, Nebr., to 12 percent for the Mississippi River below Grafton, Ill. The 5-year mean annual P inputs from manure for 1997–2002 were greater than the mean annual P inputs for the baseline period for the Arkansas River below Little Rock, Ark. (15 percent), and the Red River at Alexandria, La. (19 percent) (table 7).

Twenty-one Sites on Smaller Tributaries to the Mississippi and Atchafalaya Rivers

Twenty-one sites (table 2) are used to determine the streamflow and nutrient flux from 21 smaller subbasins of the MARB. The drainage areas of these basins range from 16,200 to 723,900 km². Most of the sites are near to the mouths of tributaries to the Mississippi River (fig. 2).

Streamflow

The estimated mean annual streamflows from 21 smaller subbasins in MARB for the 1980–1996 baseline period and the 2000–2004, 2001–2005, and 2002–2006 5-year averages are given in table 20. The 2001–2005 5-year average mean annual streamflows were less than the baseline mean annual streamflows at 8 of 21 sites, with the decreases ranging from 16 percent at the Illinois River at Valley City, Ill., to 40 percent at the Platte River at Louisville, Nebr. The 5-year average mean annual streamflows were greater than baseline mean annual streamflows at 3 of the 21 sites, with the increases ranging from 9 percent at the Wasbash River at New Harmony, Ind., to 12 percent at the Tennessee River near Paducah, Ky. The comparisons could not be made at 10 of the sites. The 2002–2006 5-year average mean annual streamflows were less than the baseline mean annual streamflows at 8 of 21 sites, with the decreases ranging from 17 percent at the Missouri River at Garrison Dam, N. Dak., to 50 percent at the Grand River near Sumner, Mo. The 5-year average mean annual streamflows were greater than baseline mean annual streamflows at 3 of the 21 sites, with the increases ranging from 10 percent at the Tennessee River near Paducah, Ky., to 15 percent at the Wabash River near New Harmony, Ind. The comparisons could not be made at 10 of the sites (table 20).

The estimated mean spring streamflows from 11 of the 21 smaller subbasins in MARB for the 1980–1996 baseline period and the 2000–2004, 2001–2005, and 2002–2006 5-year averages are given in table 21. The 11 subbasins listed in table 21 were selected because comparisons between mean spring flux for 1980–1996 and mean spring flux for 2000–2004, 2001–2005, or 2002–2006 5-year averages can be made for streamflow and at least one nutrient. The 2001–2005 5-year average mean spring streamflows were less than or equal to the baseline mean spring streamflows at 10 of 11 sites, with the decreases ranging from 0 percent at the Iowa River at Wapello, Iowa, to 39 percent at the Milk River near Nashua, Mont. The 5-year average mean spring streamflow was greater than the baseline mean spring streamflow at the Ohio River near Greenup, Ky. (16 percent). The comparison could not be made at 10 of the 21 sites. The 2002–2006 5-year average mean spring streamflows were less than the baseline mean spring streamflows at 9 of 11 sites, with the decreases ranging from 8 percent at the Missouri River at Garrison Dam, N. Dak., to 47 percent at the Platte River at Louisville, Nebr. The 5-year average mean spring streamflow was greater than the baseline mean spring streamflow at the Ohio River near Greenup, Ky. (13 percent) (table 21). The comparison could not be made at 11 of the 21 sites.

Table 20. Mean annual streamflow from 21 sites in the Mississippi-Atchafalaya River Basin, 1980–1996, 2000–2004, 2001–2005, and 2002–2006. [ND, not determined because one-half or more of the annual streamflow estimates are missing; m³/s, cubic meters per second]

Site name	Mean annual streamflow, (m³/s)			
	1980–1996	2000–2004	2001–2005	2002–2006
Allegheny River at New Kensington, Pa.	580	ND	ND	ND
Monongahela R at Braddock, Pa.	370	ND	ND	ND
Ohio River at Sewickley, Pa.	ND	ND	1,010	1,040
Kanawha River at Winfield, W. Va.	440	ND	ND	ND
Ohio River at Greenup Dam near Greenup, Ky.	2,510	2,530	2,740	2,790
Tennessee River at Highway 60 near Paducah, Ky.	1,580	1,530	1,770	1,740
Wabash River at New Harmony, Ind.	890	850	970	1,020
St. Croix River at St. Croix Falls, Wis.	145	ND	ND	ND
Minnesota River at Jordan, Minn.	186	ND	ND	ND
Mississippi River at Hastings, Minn.	ND	400	430	350
Iowa River at Wapello, Iowa	290	210	220	192
Illinois River at Valley City, Ill.	740	560	620	560
Milk River near Nashua, Mont.	14.2	6.5	ND	ND
Missouri River near Culbertson, Mont.	270	220	200	200
Yellowstone River near Sidney, Mont.	320	200	200	210
Missouri River at Garrison Dam, N. Dak.	555	487	451	460
Missouri River at Yankton, S. Dak.	ND	610	590	580
Platte River at Louisville, Nebr.	250	150	150	130
Kansas River at DeSoto, Kans.	222	ND	ND	ND
Grand River near Sumner, Mo.	150	100	110	75
Osage River below St. Thomas, Mo.	380	210	270	240

Table 21.   Spring (April, May, June) mean monthly streamflow from selected sites in the Mississippi-Atchafalaya River Basin, 1980–1996, 2000–2004, 2001–2005, and 2002–2006. [ND, not determined because one-half or more of the spring streamflow estimates are missing; m³/s, cubic meters per second]

Site name	Spring mean monthly streamflow, (m³/s)			
	1980–1996	2000–2004	2001–2005	2002–2006
Ohio River at Greenup Dam near Greenup, Ky.	3,050	3,520	3,530	3,440
Tennessee River at Highway 60 near Paducah, Ky.	1,640	1,410	1,420	1,440
Iowa River at Wapello, Iowa	430	420	430	350
Illinois River at Valley City, Ill.	1,040	920	890	840
Milk River near Nashua, Mont.	18	9.3	11	ND
Missouri River near Culbertson, Mont.	260	230	220	220
Yellowstone River near Sidney, Mont.	520	350	360	300
Missouri River at Garrison Dam, N. Dak.	520	490	460	480
Platte River at Louisville, Nebr.	360	210	230	190
Grand River near Sumner, Mo.	240	200	220	160
Osage River below St. Thomas, Mo.	580	380	420	360

Silica

The estimated mean annual silica flux from 21 smaller subbasins in MARB for the 1980–1996 baseline period and the 2000–2004, 2001–2005, and 2002–2006 5-year averages are given in table 22. Estimates of the lower and upper 95-percent confidence values for nutrient flux estimates from the 21 subbasins are not provided here, but are in Aulenbach and others (2007). The 2001–2005 5-year average mean annual silica fluxes were less than the baseline mean annual silica flux at the Missouri River near Culberston, Mont. (38 percent), and the Missouri River at Garrison Dam, N. Dak. (17 percent). The 5-year average mean annual silica fluxes were greater than the baseline mean annual silica flux at the Ohio River near Greenup, Ky. (9 percent), and the Tennessee River near Paducah, Ky. (7 percent). The comparison could not be made at 17 of the 21 sites. The 2002–2006 5-year average mean annual silica fluxes were less than the baseline mean annual silica flux at the Missouri River near Culberston, Mont. (42 percent), and the Missouri River at Garrison Dam, N. Dak. (15 percent). The 5-year average mean annual silica fluxes were greater than the baseline mean annual silica flux at the Ohio River near Greenup, Ky. (12 percent), and the Tennessee River near Paducah, Ky. (9 percent). The comparison could not be made at 17 of the 21 sites (table 22).

The estimated mean spring silica flux from 11 of the 21 smaller subbasins in MARB for the 1980–1996 baseline period and the 2000–2004, 2001–2005, and 2002–2006 5-year averages are given in table 23. The 2001–2005 5-year average mean spring silica fluxes were less than the baseline mean spring silica flux at the Tennessee River near Paducah, Ky. (40 percent); the Missouri River near Culberston, Mont. (29 percent), and the Missouri River at Garrison Dam, N. Dak. (10 percent). The 5-year average mean spring silica flux was greater than the baseline mean spring silica flux at the Ohio

River near Greenup, Ky. (10 percent). The 2002–2006 5-year average mean spring silica fluxes were less than the baseline mean spring silica flux at the Tennessee River near Paducah, Ky. (39 percent), the Missouri River near Culberston, Mont. (31 percent), and the Missouri River at Garrison Dam, N. Dak. (6 percent). The 5-year average mean spring silica flux was greater than the baseline mean spring silica flux at the Ohio River near Greenup, Ky. (5 percent). The comparisons could not be made at 17 of the 21 sites (table 23).

Total Nitrogen

The estimated mean annual total nitrogen (TN) flux from 21 smaller subbasins in MARB for the 1980–1996 baseline period and the 2000–2004, 2001–2005, and 2002–2006 5-year averages are given in table 24. The 2001–2005 5-year average mean annual TN fluxes were less than the baseline mean annual TN fluxes at 9 of 21 sites, with the decreases ranging from 6 percent at the Ohio River near Greenup, Ky., to 65 percent at the Missouri River near Culbertson, Mont. The 5-year average mean annual TN flux was greater than the baseline mean annual TN flux at the Grand River near Sumner, Mo. (80 percent). The comparison could not be made at 11 of the 21 sites. The 2002–2006 5-year average mean annual TN fluxes were less than the baseline mean annual TN fluxes at 9 of 21 sites, with the decreases ranging from 6 percent at the Ohio River near Greenup, Ky., to 65 percent at the Missouri River near Culbertson, Mont. The 5-year average mean annual TN flux was greater than the baseline mean annual TN flux at the Grand River near Sumner, Mo. (38 percent). The comparison could not be made at 11 of the 21 sites (table 24).

The estimated mean spring TN flux from 11 of the 21 smaller subbasins in MARB for the 1980–1996 baseline period and the 2000–2004, 2001–2005, and 2002–2006 5-year averages are given in table 25. The 2001–2005 5-year average

Table 22. Mean annual silica flux from 21 sites in the Mississippi-Atchafalaya River Basin, 1980–1996, 2000–2004, 2001–2005, and 2002–2006. [ND, not determined because one-half or more of the annual flux estimates are missing; t, metric tons]

Site name	Mean annual flux of silica as SiO$_2$, (t)			
	1980–1996	2000–2004	2001–2005	2002–2006
Allegheny River at New Kensington, Pa.	84,210	ND	ND	ND
Monongahela R at Braddock, Pa.	56,340	ND	ND	ND
Ohio River at Sewickley, Pa.	ND	ND	153,400	158,200
Kanawha River at Winfield, W. Va.	80,870	ND	ND	ND
Ohio River at Greenup Dam near Greenup, Ky.	456,860	440,000	498,600	510,200
Tennessee River at Highway 60 near Paducah, Ky.	225,730	191,300	241,400	246,400
Wabash River at New Harmony, Ind.	ND	315,880	402,800	422,800
St. Croix River at St. Croix Falls, Wis.	54,360	ND	ND	ND
Minnesota River at Jordan, Minn.	103,990	ND	ND	ND
Mississippi River at Hastings, Minn.	ND	ND	ND	ND
Iowa River at Wapello, Iowa	159,740	ND	ND	ND
Illinois River at Valley City, Ill.	ND	ND	ND	ND
Milk River near Nashua, Mont.	3,020	ND	ND	ND
Missouri River near Culbertson, Mont.	69,490	46,360	43,100	40,400
Yellowstone River near Sidney, Mont.	100,600	ND	ND	ND
Missouri River at Garrison Dam, N. Dak.	110,950	97,700	92,460	94,820
Missouri River at Yankton, S. Dak.	ND	157,250	151,200	146,200
Platte River at Louisville, Nebr.	210,530	ND	ND	ND
Kansas River at DeSoto, Kans.	105,550	ND	ND	ND
Grand River near Sumner, Mo.	41,690	ND	ND	ND
Osage River below St. Thomas, Mo.	63,740	ND	ND	ND

Table 23. Spring (April, May, June) mean monthly silica flux from selected sites in the Mississippi-Atchafalaya River Basin, 1980–1996, 2000–2004, 2001–2005, and 2002–2006. [ND, not determined because one-half or more of the spring flux estimates are missing; t, metric tons]

Site name	Spring mean monthly flux of silica as SiO$_2$, (t)			
	1980–1996	2000–2004	2001–2005	2002–2006
Ohio River at Greenup Dam near Greenup, Ky.	47,750	51,980	52,340	50,290
Tennessee River at Highway 60 near Paducah, Ky.	14,980	8,990	8,970	9,130
Iowa River at Wapello, Iowa	20,610	ND	ND	ND
Illinois River at Valley City, Ill.	ND	ND	ND	ND
Milk River near Nashua, Mont.	250	ND	ND	ND
Missouri River near Culbertson, Mont.	5,370	4,110	3,830	3,720
Yellowstone River near Sidney, Mont.	14,270	ND	ND	ND
Missouri River at Garrison Dam, N. Dak.	8,700	8,240	7,850	8,190
Platte River at Louisville, Nebr.	20,500	ND	ND	ND
Grand River near Sumner, Mo.	5,220	ND	ND	ND
Osage River below St. Thomas, Mo.	7,760	ND	ND	ND

Table 24. Mean annual flux of total nitrogen from 21 sites in the Mississippi-Atchafalaya River Basin, 1980–1996, 2000–2004, 2001–2005, and 2002–2006. [ND, not determined because one-half or more of the annual flux estimates are missing; TN, total nitrogen; t, metric tons]

Site name	Mean annual flux of TN as nitrogen, (t)			
	1980–1996	2000–2004	2001–2005	2002–2006
Allegheny River at New Kensington, Pa.	20,390	ND	ND	ND
Monongahela R at Braddock, Pa.	17,520	ND	ND	ND
Ohio River at Sewickley, Pa.	ND	ND	40,550	41,400
Kanawha River at Winfield, W. Va.	15,360	ND	ND	ND
Ohio River at Greenup Dam near Greenup, Ky.	131,610	116,240	123,820	124,020
Tennessee River at Highway 60 near Paducah, Ky.	48,300	35,620	41,580	41,120
Wabash River at New Harmony, Ind.	ND	134,520	152,980	157,800
St Croix River at St Croix Falls, Wis.	5,330	ND	ND	ND
Minnesota River at Jordan, Minn.	78,050	ND	ND	ND
Mississippi River at Hastings, Minn.	ND	54,460	59,850	41,370
Iowa River at Wapello, Iowa	84,030	67,850	70,040	56,080
Illinois River at Valley City, Ill.	141,390	112,600	131,470	118,730
Milk River near Nashua, Mont.	950	610	ND	ND
Missouri River near Culbertson, Mont.	8,410	3,100	2,940	2,910
Yellowstone River near Sidney, Mont.	13,510	7,070	7,150	7,890
Missouri River at Garrison Dam, N. Dak.	9,390	4,180	4,120	4,630
Missouri River at Yankton, S. Dak.	ND	8,190	7,650	6,780
Platte River at Louisville, Nebr.	37,480	23,120	24,170	20,430
Kansas River at DeSoto, Kans.	36,380	ND	ND	ND
Grand River near Sumner, Mo.	23,050	37,690	41,460	31,840
Osage River below St. Thomas, Mo.	12,820	5,500	7,630	6,760

Table 25. Spring (April, May, June) mean monthly total nitrogen flux from selected sites in the Mississippi-Atchafalaya River Basin, 1980–1996, 2000–2004, 2001–2005, and 2002–2006. [ND, not determined because one-half or more of the spring flux estimates are missing; TN, total nitrogen; t, metric tons]

Site name	Spring mean monthly flux of TN as nitrogen, (t)			
	1980–1996	2000–2004	2001–2005	2002–2006
Ohio River at Greenup Dam near Greenup, Ky.	12,620	12,080	12,050	11,560
Tennessee River at Highway 60 near Paducah, Ky.	4,200	2,460	2,410	2,430
Iowa River at Wapello, Iowa	9,730	13,200	13,190	ND
Illinois River at Valley City, Ill.	16,890	16,850	16,690	16,200
Milk River near Nashua, Mont.	90	90	110	ND
Missouri River near Culbertson, Mont.	820	350	330	330
Yellowstone River near Sidney, Mont.	1,880	1,170	1,220	690
Missouri River at Garrison Dam, N. Dak.	760	350	350	390
Platte River at Louisville, Nebr.	5,120	3,090	3,590	ND
Grand River near Sumner, Mo.	3,590	5,500	5,800	4,470
Osage River below St. Thomas, Mo.	1,770	960	1,090	960

mean spring TN fluxes were less than the baseline mean spring TN fluxes at 8 sites, with the decreases ranging from 1 percent at the Illinois River at Valley City, Ill., to 60 percent at the Missouri River near Culbertson, Mont. The 5-year average mean spring TN flux was greater than the baseline mean spring TN flux at the Iowa River at Wapello, Iowa (36 percent), the Grand River near Sumner, Mo. (62 percent), and the Milk River near Nashua, Mont. (22 percent). The comparison could not be made at 10 of the 21 sites. The 2002–2006 5-year average mean spring TN fluxes were less than the baseline mean spring TN fluxes at 7 sites, with the decreases ranging from 4 percent at the Illinois River at Valley City, Ill., to 63 percent at the Yellowstone River near Sidney, Mont. The 5-year average mean spring TN flux was greater than the baseline mean spring TN flux at the Grand River near Sumner, Mo. (25 percent), and the comparison could not be made at 13 of the 21 sites (table 25).

Nitrate

The estimated mean annual nitrate plus nitrite as N (nitrate) flux from 21 smaller subbasins in the MARB for the 1980–1996 baseline period and the 2000–2004, 2001–2005, and 2002–2006 5-year averages are given in table 26. The 2001–2005 5-year average mean annual nitrate fluxes were less than the baseline mean annual nitrate fluxes at 8 of 21 sites, with the decreases ranging from 1 percent at the Ohio River near Greenup, Ky., to 74 percent at the Missouri River near Culbertson, Mont. The 5-year average mean annual nitrate flux was greater than the baseline mean annual nitrate flux at the Grand River near Sumner, Mo. (110 percent), and the Tennessee River near Paducah, Ky. (5 percent). The comparison could not be made at 11 of the 21 sites. The 2002–2006 5-year average mean annual nitrate fluxes were less than or equal to the baseline mean annual nitrate fluxes at 8 of 21 sites, with the decreases ranging from 0 percent at the Ohio River near Greenup, Ky., to 72 percent at the Missouri River near Culbertson, Mont. The 5-year average mean annual nitrate flux was greater than the baseline mean annual nitrate flux at the Grand River near Sumner, Mo. (57 percent), and the Tennessee River near Paducah, Ky. (6 percent). The comparison could not be made at 11 of the 21 sites (table 26).

The estimated mean spring nitrate flux from 11 of the 21 smaller subbasins in MARB for the 1980–1996 baseline period and the 2000–2004, 2001–2005, and 2002–2006 5-year averages are given in table 27. The 2001–2005 5-year average mean spring nitrate fluxes were less than the baseline mean spring nitrate fluxes at 7 sites, with the decreases ranging from 6 percent at the Ohio River near Greenup, Ky., to 71 percent at the Missouri River near Culbertson, Mont. The 5-year average mean spring nitrate flux was greater than the baseline mean spring nitrate flux at the Iowa River at Wapello, Iowa (46 percent), the Grand River near Sumner, Mo. (27 percent), the Milk River near Nashua, Mont. (20 percent), and the Illinois River at Valley City, Ill. (0.5 percent). The comparison could

not be made at 10 of the 21 sites. The 2002–2006 5-year average mean spring nitrate fluxes were less than the baseline mean spring nitrate fluxes at 8 sites, with the decreases ranging from 9 percent at the Ohio River near Greenup, Ky., to 67 percent at the Missouri River near Culbertson, Mont. The 5-year average mean spring nitrate flux was greater than the baseline mean spring nitrate flux at the Iowa River at Wapello, Iowa (13 percent), and the Grand River near Sumner, Mo. (3 percent). The comparison could not be made at 11 of the 21 sites.

Total Phosphorus

The estimated mean annual total phosphorus (TP) flux from 21 smaller subbasins in MARB for the 1980–1996 baseline period and the 2000–2004, 2001–2005, and 2002–2006 5-year averages are given in table 28. The 2001–2005 5-year average mean annual TP fluxes were greater than the baseline mean annual TP fluxes at 5 of 21 sites, with the increases ranging from 16 percent at the Ohio River near Greenup, Ky., to 335 percent at the Grand River near Sumner, Mo. The 5-year average mean annual TP flux was less than the baseline mean annual TP flux at 5 of 21 sites, with the decreases ranging from 9 percent at the Yellowstone River near Sidney, Mont., and Iowa River at Wapello, Iowa, to 68 percent at the Missouri River at Garrison Dam, N. Dak. The comparison could not be made at 11 of the 21 sites. The 2002–2006 5-year average mean annual TP fluxes were greater than the baseline mean annual TP fluxes at 5 of 21 sites, with the increases ranging from 12 percent at the Illinois River at Valley City, Ill., to 254 percent at the Grand River near Sumner, Mo. The 5-year average mean annual TP flux was less than the baseline mean annual TP flux at 5 of 21 sites, with the decreases ranging from 4 percent at the Yellowstone River near Sidney, Mont., to 65 percent at the Missouri River at Garrison Dam, N. Dak. The comparison could not be made at 11 of the 21 sites.

The estimated mean spring TP flux from 11 of the 21 smaller subbasins in MARB for the 1980–1996 baseline period and the 2000–2004, 2001–2005, and 2002–2006 5-year averages are given in table 29. The 2001–2005 5-year average mean spring TP fluxes were greater than the baseline mean spring TP fluxes at 8 sites, with the increases ranging from 12 percent at the Yellowstone River near Sidney, Mont., to 435 percent at the Grand River near Sumner, Mo. The 5-year average mean spring TP flux was less than the baseline mean spring TP flux at the Missouri River at Garrison Dam, N. Dak. (67 percent), the Tennessee River near Paducah, Ky. (23 percent), and the Osage River below St. Thomas, Mo. (22 percent). The 2002–2006 5-year average mean spring TP fluxes were greater than the baseline mean spring TP fluxes at 7 sites, with the increases ranging from 3 percent at the Iowa River at Wapello, Iowa, to 313 percent at the Grand River near Sumner, Mo. The 5-year average mean spring TP flux was less than the baseline mean spring TP flux at the Missouri River at Garrison Dam, N. Dak. (63 percent), the Tennessee River

Table 26.   Mean annual flux of nitrate plus nitrite from 21 sites in the Mississippi-Atchafalaya River Basin, 1980–1996, 2000–2004, 2001–2005, and 2002–2006. [ND, not determined because one-half or more of the annual flux estimates are missing; t, metric tons]

Site name	Mean annual flux of nitrate plus nitrite as nitrogen, (t)			
	1980–1996	2000–2004	2001–2005	2002–2006
Allegheny River at New Kensington, Pa.	12,550	ND	ND	ND
Monongahela R at Braddock, Pa.	11,360	ND	ND	ND
Ohio River at Sewickley, Pa.	ND	ND	25,220	25,820
Kanawha River at Winfield, W. Va.	8,780	ND	ND	ND
Ohio River at Greenup Dam near Greenup, Ky.	75,570	70,740	74,760	75,540
Tennessee River at Highway 60 near Paducah, Ky.	21,600	18,500	22,780	22,920
Wabash River at New Harmony, Ind.	ND	106,400	122,340	126,400
St. Croix River at St. Croix Falls, Wis.	1,150	ND	ND	ND
Minnesota River at Jordan, Minn.	70,820	ND	ND	ND
Mississippi River at Hastings, Minn.	ND	40,880	45,450	31,500
Iowa River at Wapello, Iowa	68,120	57,540	58,640	46,940
Illinois River at Valley City, Ill.	108,540	90,660	107,620	94,960
Milk River near Nashua, Mont.	100	70	ND	ND
Missouri River near Culbertson, Mont.	650	150	170	180
Yellowstone River near Sidney, Mont.	3,480	2,480	2,570	2,640
Missouri River at Garrison Dam, N. Dak.	1,870	1,030	1,090	1,340
Missouri River at Yankton, S. Dak.	ND	2,090	1,820	1,370
Platte River at Louisville, Nebr.	16,480	12,880	13,270	11,730
Kansas River at DeSoto, Kans.	24,890	ND	ND	ND
Grand River near Sumner, Mo.	9,120	16,460	19,170	14,330
Osage River below St. Thomas, Mo.	5,240	2,200	3,410	3,160

Table 27.   Spring (April, May, June) mean monthly nitrate plus nitrite flux from selected sites in the Mississippi-Atchafalaya River Basin, 1980–1996, 2000–2004, 2001–2005, and 2002–2006. [ND, not determined because one-half or more of the spring flux estimates are missing; t, metric tons]

Site name	Spring mean monthly flux of nitrate plus nitrite as nitrogen, (t)			
	1980–1996	2000–2004	2001–2005	2002–2006
Ohio River at Greenup Dam near Greenup, Ky.	7,570	7,260	7,150	6,880
Tennessee River at Highway 60 near Paducah, Ky.	1,740	1,000	970	990
Iowa River at Wapello, Iowa	7,710	11,420	11,260	8,700
Illinois River at Valley City, Ill.	13,240	13,760	13,300	12,650
Milk River near Nashua, Mont.	10	10	12	ND
Missouri River near Culbertson, Mont.	58	16	17	19
Yellowstone River near Sidney, Mont.	350	220	240	220
Missouri River at Garrison Dam, N. Dak.	150	90	100	120
Platte River at Louisville, Nebr.	1,740	1,290	1,520	1,130
Grand River near Sumner, Mo.	1,240	1,430	1,570	1,280
Osage River below St. Thomas, Mo.	740	400	470	440

Table 28. Mean annual flux of total phosphorus from 21 sites in the Mississippi-Atchafalaya River Basin, 1980–1996, 2000–2004, 2001–2005, and 2002–2006. [ND, not determined because one-half or more of the annual flux estimates are missing; TP, total phosphorus; t, metric tons]

Site name	Mean annual flux of TP as phosphorus, (t)			
	1980–1996	2000–2004	2001–2005	2002–2006
Allegheny River at New Kensington, Pa.	980	ND	ND	ND
Monongahela R at Braddock, Pa.	760	ND	ND	ND
Ohio River at Sewickley, Pa.	ND	ND	2,620	2,600
Kanawha River at Winfield, W. Va.	690	ND	ND	ND
Ohio River at Greenup Dam near Greenup, Ky.	9,750	10,500	11,330	11,080
Tennessee River at Highway 60 near Paducah, Ky.	3,620	4,580	5,830	5,740
Wabash River at New Harmony, Ind.	ND	7,070	7,980	8,110
St. Croix River at St. Croix Falls, Wis.	260	ND	ND	ND
Minnesota River at Jordan, Minn.	1,340	ND	ND	ND
Mississippi River at Hastings, Minn.	ND	2,770	3,030	1,560
Iowa River at Wapello, Iowa	2,950	2,630	2,690	2,340
Illinois River at Valley City, Ill.	7,320	8,550	9,060	8,180
Milk River near Nashua, Mont.	230	250	ND	ND
Missouri River near Culbertson, Mont.	690	1,230	1,180	1,210
Yellowstone River near Sidney, Mont.	2,680	1,970	2,450	2,560
Missouri River at Garrison Dam, N. Dak.	310	100	100	110
Missouri River at Yankton, S. Dak.	ND	470	460	420
Platte River at Louisville, Nebr.	4,960	4,030	4,330	3,780
Kansas River at DeSoto, Kans.	2,720	ND	ND	ND
Grand River near Sumner, Mo.	2,850	12,020	12,400	10,080
Osage River below St. Thomas, Mo.	720	410	550	470

Table 29. Spring (April, May, June) mean monthly total phosphorus flux from selected sites in the Mississippi-Atchafalaya River Basin, 1980–1996, 2000–2004, 2001–2005, and 2002–2006. [ND, not determined because one-half or more of the spring flux estimates are missing; TP, total phosphorus; t, metric tons]

Site name	Spring mean monthly flux of TP as phosphorus, (t)			
	1980–1996	2000–2004	2001–2005	2002–2006
Ohio River at Greenup Dam near Greenup, Ky.	970	1,170	1,190	1,120
Tennessee River at Highway 60 near Paducah, Ky.	350	280	270	280
Iowa River at Wapello, Iowa	380	470	470	390
Illinois River at Valley City, Ill.	810	1,060	990	920
Milk River near Nashua, Mont.	19	42	53	ND
Missouri River near Culbertson, Mont.	70	160	150	150
Yellowstone River near Sidney, Mont.	570	510	640	590
Missouri River at Garrison Dam, N. Dak.	24	9	8	9
Platte River at Louisville, Nebr.	660	670	830	700
Grand River near Sumner, Mo.	460	2,400	2,460	1,900
Osage River below St. Thomas, Mo.	90	60	70	60

near Paducah, Ky. (20 percent), and the Osage River below St. Thomas, Mo. (33 percent); and the comparison could not be made at the Milk River near Nashua, Mont.

Orthophosphate

The estimated mean annual orthophosphate (OP) flux from 21 smaller subbasins in the MARB for the 1982–1996 baseline period and the 2000–2004, 2001–2005, and 2002–2006 5-year averages are given in table 30. The 2001–2005 5-year average mean annual OP fluxes were less than the baseline mean annual OP fluxes at 6 of 21 sites, with the decreases ranging from 7 percent at the Platte River at Louisville, Nebr., to 92 percent at the Missouri River at Garrison Dam, N. Dak. The 5-year average mean annual OP flux was greater than the baseline mean annual OP flux at the Tennessee River near Paducah, Ky. (105 percent), and the Iowa River at Wapello, Iowa (6 percent). The comparison could not be made at 13 of the 21 sites. The 2002–2006 5-year average mean annual OP fluxes were less than the baseline mean annual OP fluxes at 7 of 21 sites, with the decreases ranging from 15 percent at the Platte River at Louisville, Nebr., to 94 percent at the Missouri River at Garrison Dam, N. Dak. The 5-year average mean annual OP flux was greater than the baseline mean annual OP flux at the Tennessee River near Paducah, Ky. (103 percent), and the comparison could not be made at 13 of the 21 sites (table 30).

The estimated mean spring OP flux from 11 of the 21 smaller subbasins in MARB for the 1982–1996 baseline period and the 2000–2004, 2001–2005, and 2002–2006 5-year averages are given in table 31. The 2001–2005 5-year average mean spring OP fluxes were less than or equal to the baseline mean spring OP fluxes at 6 sites, with the decreases ranging from 0 percent at the Milk River near Nashua, Mont., to 94 percent at the Missouri River at Garrison Dam, N. Dak. The 5-year average mean spring OP flux was greater than the baseline mean spring OP flux at the Iowa River at Wapello, Iowa (26 percent), the Platte River at Louisville, Nebr. (14 percent), and the Grand River near Sumner, Mo. (5 percent); and the comparison could not be made at 12 of the 21 sites. The 2002–2006 5-year average mean spring OP fluxes were less than the baseline mean spring OP fluxes at 7 sites, with the decreases ranging from 7 percent at the Platte River at Louisville, Nebr., to 67 percent at the Missouri River near Culbertson, Mont., and the comparison could not be made at 14 of the 21 sites (table 31).

Nutrient Inputs

Estimates of mean annual inputs from fertilizer, manure, and atmospheric deposition (N only) to 21 subbasins in MARB for the 1980–1996 baseline period and the 2000–2004 5-year average are given in tables 32 for N and 33 for P. The 5-year average annual N inputs from fertilizer for 2000–2004 were greater than the baseline period average annual N inputs from fertilizer in 17 of 21 subbasins, with the increases

ranging from 0.1 percent at the Monongahela River at Braddock, Pa., to 113 percent at the Missouri River at Yankton, S. Dak. The 5-year average annual N inputs from fertilizer for 2000–2004 were less than the baseline period average annual N inputs from fertilizer in 4 of 21 subbasins, with the decreases ranging from 2 percent at the Allegheny River at New Kensington, Pa., to 6 percent at the Tennessee River near Paducah, Ky. (table 32). The average annual N inputs from manure for 1997–2002 were less than the baseline period average annual N inputs from manure in 15 of the 21 subbasins, with the decreases ranging from 1 percent at the Milk River near Nashua, Mont., to 30 percent at the Osage River below St. Thomas, Mo. The average annual N inputs from manure for 1997–2002 were equal to or greater than the N inputs for the baseline period in 6 of 21 subbasins, with the increases ranging from 0 percent at the Missouri River at Yankton, S. Dak., to 11 percent at the Tennessee River near Paducah, Ky. The 5-year average N inputs from atmospheric deposition for 2000–2004 were greater than the baseline period average annual N inputs from atmospheric deposition in 15 of the 21 subbasins, with the increases ranging from 1 percent at the Wabash River at New Harmony, Ind., to 22 percent at both the Missouri River at Garrison Dam, N. Dak., and the Missouri River at Yankton, S. Dak. The 5-year average annual N inputs from atmospheric deposition for 2000–2004 were less than the N inputs for the baseline period in 6 of 21 subbasins with the decreases ranging from 3 percent at the Kanawha River at Winfield, W. Va., to 18 percent at the Monongahela River at Braddock, Pa. (table 32).

The 5-year average P inputs from fertilizer for 2000–2004 were less than the baseline period average annual P input from fertilizer in 11 of the 21 subbasins, with the decreases ranging from 3 percent at the Grand River near Sumner, Mo., to 36 percent at the Monongahela River at Braddock, Pa. The 5-year average P inputs from fertilizer for 2000–2004 were greater than the P inputs for the baseline period in 10 of the 21 subbasins, with the increases ranging from 3 percent at the Mississippi River at Hastings, Minn., to 59 percent at the Missouri River at Yankton, S. Dak. (table 33). The average annual P inputs from manure for 1997–2002 were less than the baseline period average annual P inputs from manure in 15 of the 21 subbasins, with the decreases ranging from 0.1 percent at the Missouri River at Yankton, S. Dak., to 26 percent at the Illinois River at Valley City, Ill. The 5-year average annual P inputs from manure for 1997–2002 were greater than the P inputs for the baseline period in 6 of the 21 subbasins, with the increases ranging from 1 percent at the Platte River at Louisville, Nebr., to 19 percent at the Minnesota River at Jordan, Minn.

Statistical Trend Analysis

Even if no changes in nutrient sources, management practices, or major land-use patterns occurred during the 1980–2006 study period, annual nutrient fluxes would be expected

Table 30. Mean annual flux of orthophosphate from 21 sites in the Mississippi-Atchafalaya River Basin, 1982–1996, 2000–2004, 2001–2005, and 2002–2006. [ND, not determined because one-half or more of the annual flux estimates are missing; OP, orthophosphate; t, metric tons]

Site name	Mean annual flux of OP as phosphorus, (t)			
	1982–1996	2000–2004	2001–2005	2002–2006
Allegheny River at New Kensington, Pa.	ND	ND	ND	ND
Monongahela R at Braddock, Pa.	130	ND	ND	ND
Ohio River at Sewickley, Pa.	ND	ND	240	240
Kanawha River at Winfield, W. Va.	190	ND	ND	ND
Ohio River at Greenup Dam near Greenup, Ky.	ND	940	880	830
Tennessee River at Highway 60 near Paducah, Ky.	1,310	2,160	2,680	2,660
Wabash River at New Harmony, Ind.	ND	2,840	3,570	3,540
St. Croix River at St. Croix Falls, Wis.	60	ND	ND	ND
Minnesota River at Jordan, Minn.	650	ND	ND	ND
Mississippi River at Hastings, Minn.	ND	1,120	1,160	800
Iowa River at Wapello, Iowa	1,360	1,240	1,440	1,070
Illinois River at Valley City, Ill.	ND	3,410	3,700	3,460
Milk River near Nashua, Mont.	10	4	ND	ND
Missouri River near Culbertson, Mont.	150	50	50	44
Yellowstone River near Sidney, Mont.	160	44	42	49
Missouri River at Garrison Dam, N. Dak.	210	14	16	12
Missouri River at Yankton, S. Dak.	ND	57	48	25
Platte River at Louisville, Nebr.	1,440	1,210	1,340	1,230
Kansas River at DeSoto, Kans.	1,200	ND	ND	ND
Grand River near Sumner, Mo.	260	170	180	150
Osage River below St. Thomas, Mo.	330	100	110	100

Table 31. Spring (April, May, June) mean monthly orthophosphate flux from selected sites in the Mississippi-Atchafalaya River Basin, 1982–1996, 2000–2004, 2001–2005, and 2002–2006. [ND, not determined because one-half or more of the spring flux estimates are missing; OP, orthophosphate; t, metric tons]

Site name	Spring mean monthly flux of OP as phosphorus, (t)			
	1982–1996	2000–2004	2001–2005	2002–2006
Ohio River at Greenup Dam near Greenup, Ky.	ND	80	70	60
Tennessee River at Highway 60 near Paducah, Ky.	70	70	60	60
Iowa River at Wapello, Iowa	190	230	240	160
Illinois River at Valley City, Ill.	ND	330	320	310
Milk River near Nashua, Mont.	1	1	1	ND
Missouri River near Culbertson, Mont.	12	5	4	4
Yellowstone River near Sidney, Mont.	24	11	10	9
Missouri River at Garrison Dam, N. Dak.	17	1	1	ND
Platte River at Louisville, Nebr.	140	120	160	130
Grand River near Sumner, Mo.	38	37	40	30
Osage River below St. Thomas, Mo.	38	14	15	14

Table 32.   Mean annual nitrogen inputs to 21 subbasins in the Mississippi-Atchafalaya River Basin. [N, nitrogen; t, metric tons]

Site name and subbasin number(s)	Mean annual N input from fertilizer, (t)		Mean annual N input from manure, (t)		Mean annual N input from atmospheric deposition, (t)	
	1980–1996	2000–2004	1982–1996	1997–2002	1985–1996	2000–2004
Allegheny River at New Kensington, Pa. (1)	10,934	10,732	16,718	14,419	20,825	19,920
Monongahela R at Braddock, Pa. (2)	4,589	4,593	10,015	9,630	12,750	10,509
Ohio River at Sewickley, Pa. (1,2,3)	16,010	16,052	27,341	24,550	34,524	31,291
Kanawha River at Winfield, W. Va. (4)	8,355	9,497	17,840	17,876	14,711	14,337
Ohio River at Greenup Dam near Greenup, Ky. (1,2,3,4,5)	98,018	98,990	100,816	94,384	95,514	90,557
Tennessee River at Highway 60 near Paducah, Ky. (6)	100,455	94,048	113,688	126,052	48,289	49,689
Wabash River at New Harmony, Ind. (7)	420,320	422,138	87,065	70,799	44,415	44,799
St. Croix River at St. Croix Falls, Wis. (8)	10,141	10,251	9,691	7,155	7,377	8,650
Minnesota River at Jordan, Minn. (9)	197,461	233,591	58,977	63,833	20,523	22,332
Mississippi River at Hastings, Minn. (9,10)	283,573	325,986	115,214	111,959	42,566	48,221
Iowa River at Wapello, Iowa (11)	133,779	128,690	46,036	39,402	11,381	11,709
Illinois River at Valley City, Ill. (12)	309,303	297,632	44,406	32,323	26,884	25,329
Milk River near Nashua, Mont. (13)	11,967	16,473	10,526	10,430	4,285	5,029
Missouri River near Culbertson, Mont. (13,14)	75,037	102,954	75,668	72,723	21,440	25,672
Yellowstone River near Sidney, Mont. (15)	42,756	70,185	67,670	65,833	18,951	22,901
Missouri River at Garrison Dam, N. Dak. (13,14,15,16)	141,525	229,496	163,724	160,200	48,167	58,841
Missouri River at Yankton, S. Dak. (13,14,15,16,17)	216,825	462,847	358,865	358,898	108,308	132,279
Platte River at Louisville, Nebr. (18)	395,663	428,505	251,747	262,952	62,719	70,292
Kansas River at DeSoto, Kans. (19)	486,239	518,490	179,904	182,543	59,202	65,736
Grand River near Sumner, Mo. (20)	39,931	40,813	28,725	27,409	9,419	9,972
Osage River below St. Thomas, Mo. (21)	71,488	83,120	59,144	41,491	19,107	20,260

to vary substantially from year to year in response to natural variability in climate and hence rainfall-runoff, groundwater flow, and streamflow. Multiyear dry or wet periods can occur in different subbasins during different times, changing the volume and chemical composition of streamflow from the sub-basins. Therefore, it is necessary to determine if the generally lower fluxes of nitrogen, phosphorus, and silica to the Gulf of Mexico during 1997–2006, compared with the baseline period (1980–1996) (fig. 3), reflect a true change toward improving conditions rather than a short-term anomaly.

The KW test was used to test for a significant differ-ence between the annual streamflow and nutrient fluxes for the baseline (1980–1996) period and the recent (2000–2006) period. The test results for the Mississippi River at Thebes, Ill. (table 34), indicated mildly significant (p = 0.1 to 0.05) to moderately significant (p = 0.05 to 0.01) differences between the two time periods for annual streamflow and annual fluxes of TN, nitrate, and OP. The KW test is two-sided, but the significant results all were associated with lower values for the latter period. For the Ohio River near Grand Chain, Ill., there was only one mildly significant result (OP). For the Mississippi River near St. Francisville, La., and the Atchafa-laya River at Melville, La., there were mildly to moderately

significant changes for streamflow, TN, nitrate, and OP (Saint Francisville only).

There are a number of issues that need to be considered when interpreting the trends indicated in table 34 for the annual nutrient fluxes. The KW test assumes annual flux esti-mates for different years are uncorrelated and have constant variance (Helsel and Hirsch, 2002); however, closer examina-tion of the data indicated that one or both of these assumptions may be violated for all of the sites. The probable cause for serial correlation and(or) nonconstant variance of the annual flux estimates is variable streamflow conditions. Streamflows tend to be correlated and highly variable from year to year, and because much of the variability in annual nutrient flux is due to variability in streamflow, annual nutrient fluxes also tend to be correlated and highly variable. Therefore, the annual flux estimates were regressed on annual streamflow and the residu-als from the regression model were examined for trends using the KW test. A significant trend in the residuals indicates that a change in nutrient fluxes occurred even after correcting for variable streamflow conditions.

In most cases, the test results for the residuals differed substantially from the results for the raw data (table 34). For the Mississippi River at Thebes, Ill., the test results

Table 33. Mean annual phosphorus inputs to 21 subbasins in the Mississippi-Atchafalaya River Basin. [P, phosphorus; t, metric tons]

Site name and subbasin number(s)	Mean annual P input from fertilizer, (t)		Mean annual P input from manure, (t)	
	1980–1996	2000–2004	1982–1996	1997–2002
Allegheny River at New Kensington, Pa. (1)	3,537	2,359	3,495	3,096
Monongahela R at Braddock, Pa. (2)	1,489	957	2,639	2,539
Ohio River at Sewickley, Pa. (1,2,3)	5,158	3,486	6,284	5,766
Kanawha River at Winfield, W. Va. (4)	2,523	2,342	5,071	5,163
Ohio River at Greenup Dam near Greenup, Ky. (1,2,3,4,5)	24,759	19,262	25,679	24,447
Tennessee River at Highway 60 near Paducah, Ky. (6)	25,868	22,280	33,589	37,438
Wabash River at New Harmony, Ind. (7)	87,787	68,988	30,812	25,413
St. Croix River at St. Croix Falls, Wis. (8)	2,039	1,737	2,169	1,741
Minnesota River at Jordan, Minn. (9)	35,985	41,133	19,032	22,714
Mississippi River at Hastings, Minn. (9,10)	51,801	53,218	33,147	35,327
Iowa River at Wapello, Iowa (11)	20,531	19,290	16,607	14,867
Illinois River at Valley City, Ill. (12)	59,059	47,447	15,302	11,274
Milk River near Nashua, Mont. (13)	3,172	3,439	3,308	3,244
Missouri River near Culbertson, Mont. (13,14)	19,704	21,332	23,171	22,356
Yellowstone River near Sidney, Mont. (15)	8,019	10,180	20,258	19,763
Missouri River at Garrison Dam, N. Dak. (13,14,15,16)	32,058	40,740	49,623	48,519
Missouri River at Yankton, S. Dak. (13,14,15,16,17)	50,665	80,430	109,161	109,027
Platte River at Louisville, Nebr. (18)	38,660	57,618	75,615	76,258
Kansas River at DeSoto, Kans. (19)	52,078	67,861	55,501	53,681
Grand River near Sumner, Mo. (20)	7,088	6,886	9,379	8,924
Osage River below St. Thomas, Mo. (21)	11,628	13,170	17,892	20,228

Table 34. P-values from Kruskal-Wallis test for difference between annual fluxes for 1980–1996 and 2000–2006, using raw data and residuals from a regression of annual flux on annual flow. [p-values are dimensionless; NA, not applicable]

Site name and data type	Mississippi River at Thebes, Ill.		Ohio River at Dam 53 near Grand Chain, Ill.		Mississippi River near St. Francisville, La.		Atchafalaya River at Melville, La.	
	Raw	Residuals	Raw	Residuals	Raw	Residuals	Raw	Residuals
Streamflow	0.045	NA	0.567	NA	0.098	NA	0.092	NA
Total nitrogen as N	0.033	0.465	0.427	0.357	0.006	0.020	0.017	0.120
Nitrate plus nitrite as N	0.057	0.546	0.546	0.634	0.045	0.266	0.049	0.589
Total phosphorus	0.546	0.008	0.162	0.001	0.799	0.589	0.680	0.215
Orthophosphate	0.015	0.568	0.062	0.026	0.022	0.972	0.217	0.860

after accounting for streamflow differences were completely reversed from the results for the raw data, and only TP indicated a significant difference between the two periods (with higher fluxes for the recent period). Conflicting results also occurred for the remaining sites. At the Mississippi River near St. Francisville, La., there is a significant difference between the two periods for TN (with lower fluxes for the recent period).

The components of the parametric time series model (Vecchia, 2005) for flux are shown for TP for the Ohio River near Grand Chain, Ill. (fig. 6). In the top panel, the raw (unadjusted) flux estimates are shown along with a line showing the mean plus the seasonal anomaly ($M_F + SEAS_F$, eq. 3). The middle panel shows the seasonally adjusted flux ($log\ F(t) - SEAS_F$) and the annual anomaly ($M_F + ANN_F$). Both the seasonal and annual anomalies represent "natural" variability in the flux values as a result of variation in streamflow conditions. Both anomalies explain a large part of the overall variability of the flux estimates. The seasonal anomaly varies over almost two orders of magnitude (2 base-10 log cycles), and the annual anomaly varies over one order of magnitude. The annual anomaly is particularly important when considering annual flux estimates because aggregating daily fluxes on an annual scale would not smooth out such variation. The bottom panel of figure 6 shows the fluxes after removing the seasonal and annual anomalies and using the Kalman filter (Vecchia, 2005) to remove serial correlation between daily fluxes [$log\ F(t) - ANN_F - SEAS_F - Pr\{ HFV_F \}$, where $Pr\{ HFV_F \}$ is the predicted value of HFV_F obtained using the Kalman filter algorithm], along with a line showing the fitted trend ($M_F + TREND_F$). In this case, there was a highly significant increase from 1995 to 2000 (an estimated increase of 30 percent, with a p-value less than 0.0001). Although the trend is highly significant both from a statistical and practical standpoint, note that it is much smaller in magnitude than the annual anomaly. Therefore, interannual streamflow-related variability in TP flux is far greater than the fitted trend. This shows the importance of properly accounting for interannual variability in these data before analyzing for trends.

Results of the trend analysis using the time series model are given in table 35. These trends presumably reflect changes occurring in the basins that are unrelated to trends or variability in streamflow. Although trend analyses were done for the 1980–2006 time period, significant trends were reported only for two 5-year time periods, 1985–1989, and 1995–1999. Evaluating causes for the statistical trends is beyond the scope of this report. Trends in silica are not included because no significant trends were found for that nutrient for any time period at any of the sites.

There were significant decreases in TN flux for 1985–1989 for all four sites (table 35). The trends ranged from an estimated decrease of 10 percent at the Mississippi River at Thebes, Ill., to an estimated decrease of 25 percent at the Ohio River at Grand Chain, Ill. There was a significant increase of 18 percent in TN flux for the Ohio River at Grand Chain,

Ill., for 1995–1999, but none of the other sites had significant trends for this or other time periods (trends were considered significant if the p-value was less than or equal to 0.05).

There was only one significant trend in nitrate, an estimated decrease of 15 percent for 1985–1989 for the Atchafalaya River at Melville, La. (table 35). The lack of significant trends for nitrate indicates that the downward trends in TN flux probably resulted from decreases in organic nitrogen or ammonia, as only the Atchafalaya River at Melville, La., had decreasing nitrate fluxes as well. There was unanimous agreement among the sites with regard to trends in ammonium (table 35). Large and significant decreases of 46 to 57 percent occurred during 1985–1989 for all four sites. Apparently, the downward TN trends were caused at least in part by decreases in ammonium.

There was general agreement among the sites with regard to trends in TP flux as well. Significant increases from 11 to 30 percent occurred for all four sites during 1995–1999. The largest increase was for the Ohio River at Grand Chain, Ill., and the smallest increases were for the Mississippi River near St. Francisville, La., and Atchafalaya River at Melville, La. Similar increases occurred for orthophosphate during 1995–1999 except for the Ohio River at Grand Chain, Ill., for which the significant increase in TP flux was not matched by an increase in orthophosphate flux. The discrepancy between total phosphorus and orthophosphate for this site may indicate a difference in the processes affecting TP and orthophosphate. However, a lack of a significant trend does not necessarily imply that a trend did not occur.

The fitted trends for TN, nitrate, and TP flux for the Mississippi River near St. Francisville, La., and the Atchafalaya River at Melville, La. are shown in figures 7 and 8. The points are the adjusted and filtered fluxes, as described in the previous discussion (fig. 6, bottom panel). With the exception of dissolved nitrate, the trends for these two sites are nearly identical (table 35).

It appears that very little of the decrease in annual nutrient fluxes that has occurred between the 1980–1996 baseline period and more recent years can be attributed to recent management actions or other human-controlled activities in the MARB. Although simple statistical tests show a significant decrease in TN at the Mississippi at St. Francisville, La. (table 34), the more complex statistical trend analysis indicates that the change in TN flux predates recent attempts to limit nutrient flux to the Gulf of Mexico. The downward trends in TN, nitrate, ammonium, and orthophosphate that were detected at either the Mississippi River near St. Francisville, La., or the Atchafalaya River at Melville, La., largely occurred prior to 1990 (figs. 7 and 8, table 35). In more recent years no trends were detected for TN, nitrate, and ammonium, and an upward trend was detected for TP and orthophosphate. Others have recently reported on nutrient trends in United States streams at different sites and for different time periods (Rebich and Demcheck, 2007; Sprague and Lorenz, 2009). The trend results presented here

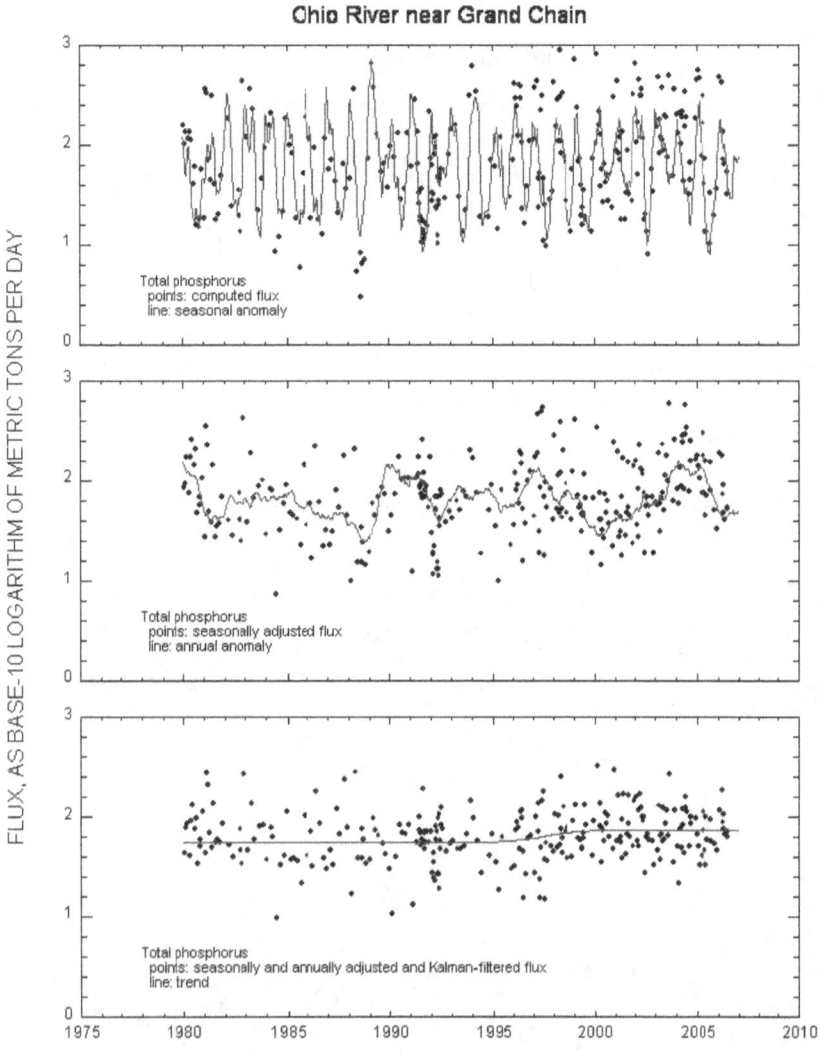

Figure 6. Seasonal anomaly, annual anomaly, and trend for daily total phosphorus flux for the Ohio River near Grand Chain, Ill., for 1980–2006.

Table 35. Fitted trends (as percent change over a 5-year period) in daily nutrient fluxes as based on the time series analysis.
[p-values shown in parentheses; NT, no trend detected]

Site name and data type	Mississippi River at Thebes, Ill.		Ohio River at Dam 53 near Grand Chain, Ill.		Mississippi River near St. Francisville, La.		Atchafalaya River at Melville, La.	
	1985–1989	1995–1999	1985–1989	1995–1999	1985–1989	1995–1999	1985–1989	1995–1999
Total nitrogen as N	−10 (0.008)	NT	−25 (0.000)	+18 (0.001)	−23 (0.000)	NT	−24 (0.000)	NT
Nitrate plus nitrite as N	NT	NT	NT	NT	NT	NT	−15 (0.007)	NT
Ammonium as N	−52 (0.000)	NT	−46 (0.000)	NT	−57 (0.000)	NT	−57 (0.000)	NT
Total phosphorus	NT	+16 (0.013)	NT	+30 (0.000)	NT	+11 (0.033)	NT	+11 (0.041)
Orthophosphate	NT	+9 (0.048)	NT	NT	−17 (0.010)	+15 (0.016)	−19 (0.004)	+14 (0.039)

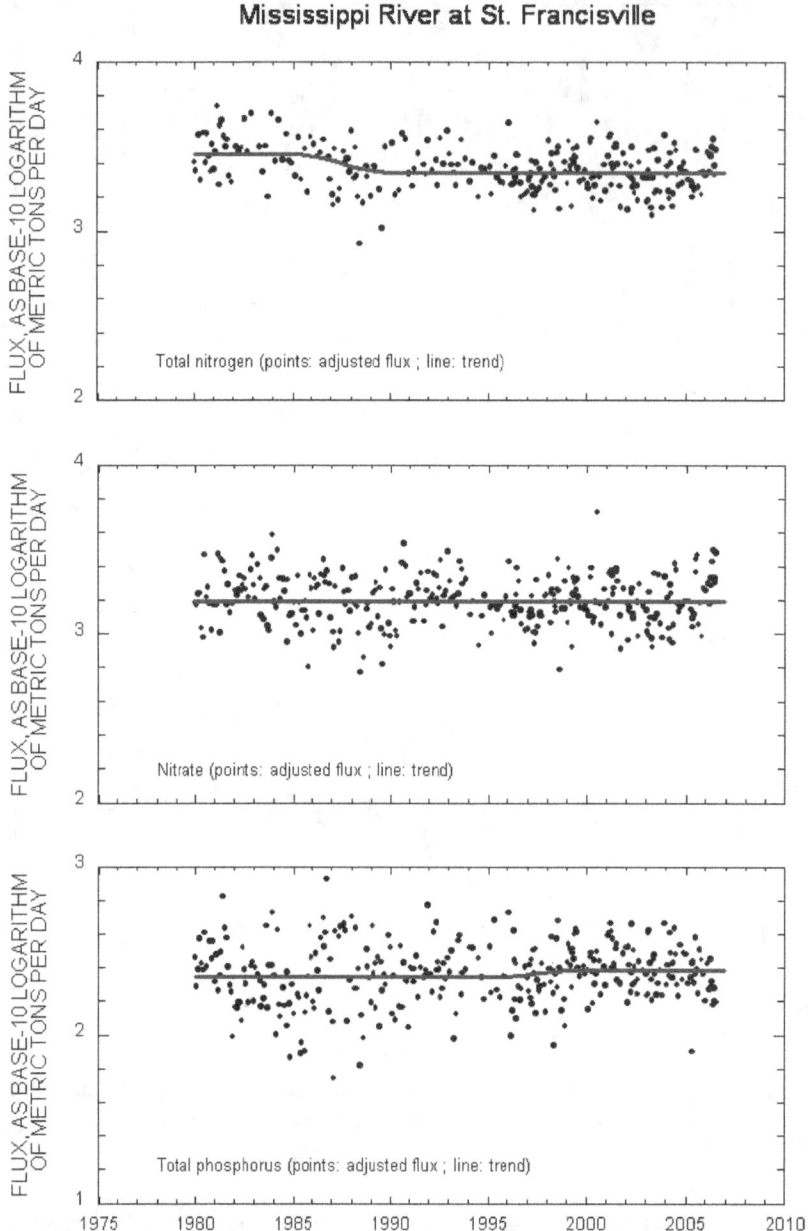

Figure 7. Fitted trends in daily fluxes of total nitrogen, nitrate, and total phosphorus for 1980–2006 for the Mississippi River at St. Francisville, La. [points are annually and seasonally adjusted and Kalman-filtered daily flux estimates (Vecchia, 2005)]

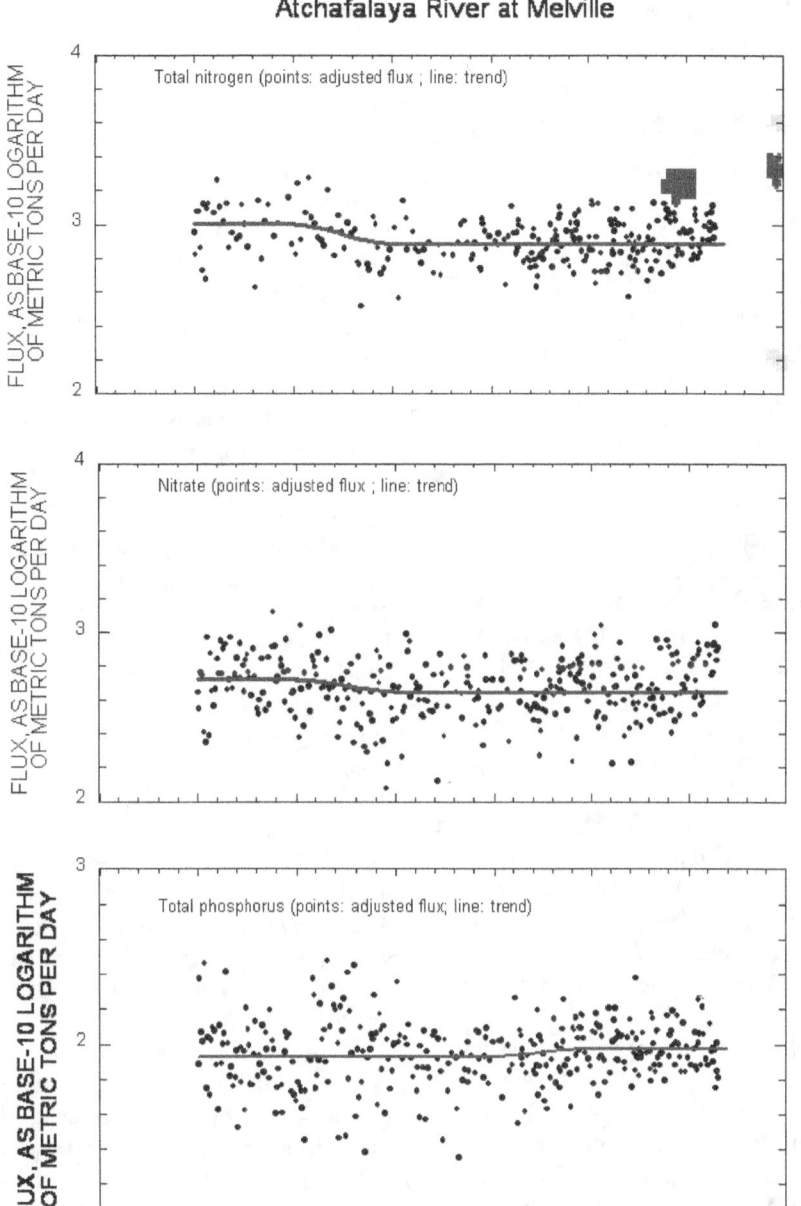

Figure 8. Fitted trends in daily fluxes of total nitrogen, nitrate, and total phosphorus for 1980–2006 for the Atchafalaya River at Melville, La. [data points are annually and seasonally adjusted and Kalman-filtered daily flux estimates (Vecchia, 2005)]

are consistent with those presented by Rebich and Demcheck (2007) for 1993-2004 at 115 sites in the south-central United States and by Sprague and Lorenz (2009) for 1993-2003 at 171 sites across the United States.

Patterns in Streamflow, Nutrient Inputs, and Nutrient Flux

This report provides updated estimates of the annual and monthly flux of nutrients from the MARB to the Gulf of Mexico and at numerous locations with the MARB. Estimates of nutrient flux for the baseline period (1980–1996) were recalculated and differ some from those reported by Goolsby and others (1999). These differences result primarily from four factors: (1) for the Goolsby report annual flux was calculated for calendar years, and for this report annual flux is calculated for water years; (2) for the Goosby report the entire period of record is used for model calibration, and for this report a 10-year moving period is used for model calibration; (3) for the Goolsby report the model was used to extrapolate fluxes across data gaps, and for this report years with significant data gaps are omitted; and (4) for the Goolsby report nondetects were assigned a value of one-half the laboratory reporting level, and for this report AMLE is used to infer censored sample concentrations from the distribution of sample concentration above the reporting level.

Mean annual streamflow from the Mississippi and Atchafalaya Rivers to the Gulf of Mexico has decreased from the 1980–1996 baseline period by about 10 percent. The decreases in mean annual streamflow were widespread, occurring in 9 of 11 major subbasins during the 2002–2006 5-year period. Mean spring streamflows changed similarly. Spring streamflow from 1997–2007 to the Gulf of Mexico has decreased by about 12 percent from the 1980–1996 baseline period. Decreases in mean spring streamflow were observed in 8 of 11 major subbasins during 2002–2006.

With the decreases in streamflow came decreases in the flux of most nutrients. The 5-year average mean annual flux of silica to the Gulf of Mexico has decreased from the 1980–1996 baseline period on average by about 18 percent. The decrease in annual silica is greater (on a percentage basis) than the decrease in mean annual streamflow. The decreases in mean annual silica flux were widespread, occurring in 8 of 10 major subbasins during the 2002–2006 5-year period. Mean spring silica flux changed similarly. Spring silica flux to the Gulf of Mexico has decreased by about 20 percent from the 1980–1996 baseline period, which is greater than the decrease in mean spring streamflow. Decreases in mean spring silica flux were observed in all 10 of the major subbasins during 2002–2006.

The 5-year average mean annual flux of TN to the Gulf of Mexico has decreased from the 1980–1996 baseline period by about 22 percent, which is greater than the decrease in mean annual streamflow. The decreases in mean annual TN flux were widespread, occurring in all 11 major subbasins during the 2002–2006 5-year period. Mean spring TN flux changed similarly. Spring TN flux to the Gulf of Mexico has decreased by about 18 percent from the 1980–1996 baseline period, which is greater than the decrease in mean spring streamflow. Decreases in mean spring TN flux were observed in 10 of 11 major subbasins during 2002–2006.

The 5-year average mean annual flux of nitrate to the Gulf of Mexico has decreased from the 1980–1996 baseline period by about 15 percent, which is greater than the decrease in mean annual streamflow. The decreases in mean annual nitrate flux were widespread, occurring in 8 of 11 major subbasins during the 2002–2006 5-year period. Mean spring nitrate flux changed similarly. Spring nitrate flux to the Gulf of Mexico has decreased by about 10 percent from the 1980–1996 baseline period, which is about the same as the decrease in mean spring streamflow. Decreases in mean spring nitrate flux were observed in 8 of 11 major subbasins during 2002–2006.

The 5-year average mean annual flux of TP to the Gulf of Mexico has increased from the 1980–1996 baseline period by about 4 percent, even though streamflow decreased. The increases in mean annual TP flux were neither widespread nor consistent between 5-year periods. For example, the 2001–2005 5-year average mean annual TP fluxes were greater than the baseline mean annual TP fluxes at 7 of 11 sites, whereas mean annual TP fluxes decreased in 9 of 11 major subbasins during the 2002–2006 5-year period. Mean spring TP flux behaved similarly. Spring TP flux to the Gulf of Mexico has increased by about 7 percent from the 1980–1996 baseline period, even though streamflow decreased. The 2001–2005 5-year average mean spring TP fluxes were greater than the baseline mean spring TP fluxes at 8 of 11 sites, whereas the mean spring TP flux decreased in 6 of 11 major subbasins during 2002–2006.

The 5-year average mean annual flux of orthophosphate to the Gulf of Mexico has decreased from the 1982–1996 baseline period by about 11 percent, which is about the same as the decrease in streamflow. The decreases in mean annual orthophosphate flux were widespread, occurring in 9 of 10 major subbasins during the 2002–2006 5-year period. Mean spring orthophosphate flux changed similarly. Spring orthophosphate flux to the Gulf of Mexico has decreased by about 5 percent from the 1982–1996 baseline period, which is less than the decrease in streamflow. Decreases in mean spring orthophosphate flux were observed in 8 of 9 major subbasins during 2002–2006.

Most major inputs of nutrients in the MARB have increased or remained about the same. The 5-year average mean annual inputs to the MARB of nitrogen from fertilizer have increased from the 1980–1996 baseline period by about 12 percent, and annual inputs of phosphorus from fertilizer have increased by about 2 percent. The 5-year average mean annual inputs of nitrogen from atmospheric deposition have increased from the 1980–1996 baseline period by about 7 percent. The 5-year average mean annual inputs of nitrogen from manure have decreased from the 1980–1996 baseline period by less than 1 percent, and annual inputs of phosphorus from manure have increased by less than 1 percent. There was a decrease in point-source inputs of both N and P between the baseline period and the recent period; however, the human population in the basin increased from about 69.4 million in 1990 to about 76.3 million in 2000 (U.S. Census Bureau, 2008). Increases in nutrient inputs from fertilizer are expected to continue. Nitrogen inputs from fertilizer in the United States are forecast to grow at a rate of between 1.7 and 1.8 percent per year between 2010 and 2030, and phosphorus inputs from fertilizer are forecast to grow at a rate of between 0.59 and 0.67 percent per year during that same time period (Zhang and Zhang, 2007). Howarth and others (2002) also forecast an increase in nitrogen fertilizer use between 2000 and 2030, unless Americans change to a "Mediterranean diet."

The reductions in nitrogen flux have not resulted in corresponding decreases in the size of the Gulf of Mexico hypoxic zone. The size of the hypoxic zone has increased by about 30 percent from an average of about 11,400 square kilometers during the baseline period to about 14,600 square kilometers during the 2003–2007 5-year period (fig. 9). The reasons for this are not clear but could be due to the nature of nutrient delivery (Dodds, 2006; Turner and others, 2008). The percentage of the mean annual flux of TN as nitrate to the Gulf of Mexico has increased steadily from about 55 percent in the 1980s to about 70 percent in recent years (fig. 10), and the portion of spring flux of TN as nitrate has increased similarly.

TP flux (both annual and springtime) has increased, and it may be that the hypoxic zone is responding more to TP flux than was previously thought (Howarth and Marino, 2006; Sylvan and others, 2006; Rabalais and others, 2007; Scavia and Donnelly, 2007). The percentage of the mean annual and mean spring flux of TP as orthophosphate to the Gulf has also changed, decreasing from about 30 percent in the 1980s to about 25 percent in recent years. The ratio of TN flux to TP flux appears not to have changed significantly from the baseline period at about 15 to 1 (fig. 10), even though the flux of TN has decreased and the flux of TP has stayed the same or increased. The potential effects of TP on Gulf of Mexico hypoxia were sufficient to cause the only change between 2001 and 2008 to the three goals of the Gulf Hypoxia Action Plans (Mississippi River/Gulf of Mexico Watershed Nutrient Task Force, 2001; 2008): the addition of "and phosphorus" to the last sentence of the Coastal Goal.

Springtime (April, May, and June) nutrient-flux estimates were divided by the size of the hypoxic zone (measured in mid-July) to calculate estimates of the nutrient flux required per unit increase in the size of the hypoxic zone (fig. 11). During the baseline period approximately 50 t of TN (or 33 t of nitrate) was delivered to the gulf for each square kilometer of hypoxic zone. For the 2003–2007 5-year period, those inputs were reduced to 31 t and 22 t, respectively. The change was less striking for TP and orthophosphate (fig. 11). During the baseline period approximately 3.8 t of TP (or 1.1 t of

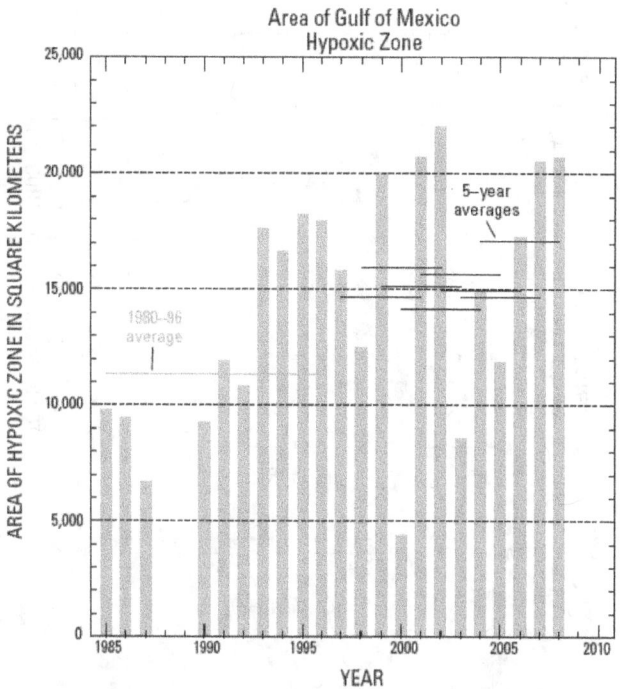

Figure 9. Area of Gulf of Mexico hypoxic zone in late July, 1985–2008 (from Rabalais and others, 2007; N. Rabalais, Louisiana Universities Marine Consortium, written commun., 2008).

OP) was delivered to the gulf of each square kilometer of the hypoxic zone that formed. For the 2003–2007 5-year period, those inputs were reduced to 3.0 t of TP and 0.8 t of OP. Using these simple ratios, it is estimated that reducing the average size of the hypoxic zone to 5,000 km^2 would require reducing the springtime delivery of TN to the gulf to about 155,000 t, nitrate to about 110,000 t, TP to about 15,000 t, and OP to about 4,000 t. These amounts are less than the 2003–2007 mean spring fluxes (table 5) by 64, 64, 63, and 62 percent, respectively.

Streamflow and nutrient fluxes for the major subbasins of the MARB are summarized in tables 3-5, 8-19. Figure 12 shows the relative contributions of five major subbasins to the total streamflow, TN flux, and TP flux to the Gulf of Mexico for 1980–2006. The percentages are calculated by dividing the streamflow or nutrient flux from the subbasin by the "to-the-Gulf" streamflow or nutrient flux. The calculation assumes there are no in-stream losses of water or nutrients and does not account for inputs or losses from the Lower Mississippi (subbasin 10 in figure 1). The five subbasins are (1) the Mississippi River at Thebes, Ill. (less the inputs from the Missouri River at Hermann, Mo.)(subbasin numbers 1, 2, and 5 in figure 1), (2) the Ohio River at Dam 53 near Grand Chain, Ill. (subbasin numbers 6 and 7), (3) the Missouri River at Hermann, Mo. (subbasin numbers 3 and 4), (4) the Arkansas River below Little Rock, Ark. (subbasin number 8), and (5) the Red River at Alexandria, La. (subbasin number 9).

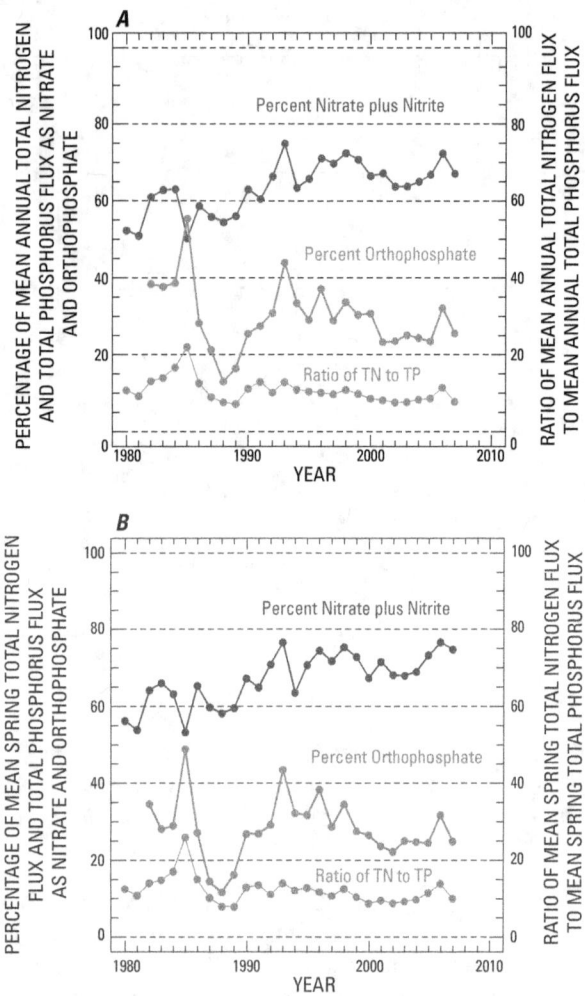

Figure 10. Percentage of mean annual (A) and mean spring (B) total nitrogen flux as nitrate, total phosphorus flux as orthophosphate, and the ratio of total nitrogen flux to total phosphorus flux in water delivered to the Gulf of Mexico.

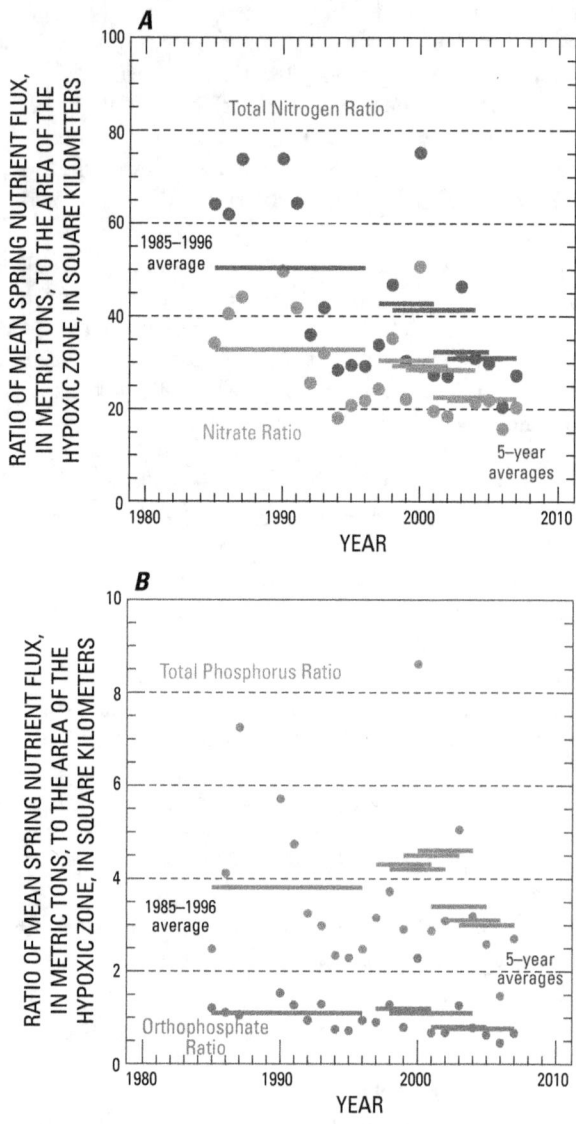

Figure 11. Ratio of mean spring flux of (A) total nitrogen and nitrate and (B) total phosphorus and orthophosphate to the area of the Gulf of Mexico hypoxic zone in water delivered to the Gulf of Mexico.

The sum of streamflow from the five subbasins as a percentage of total streamflow to the Gulf of Mexico ranged from 73 to 90 percent and averaged 81 percent for the 1980–2006 period (fig. 12). Streamflow from the Ohio River Basin was always larger than streamflow from the other four subbasins and averaged 40 percent of the to-the-Gulf total for 1980–2006. Streamflow from the Ohio River Basin as a percentage of the to-the-Gulf total averaged 38 percent for the 1980–1996 baseline period; and 42, 43, and 47 percent for the 2000–2004, 2001–2005, and 2002–2006 5-year periods, respectively. Streamflow from the Upper Mississippi River Basin as a percentage of the to-the-Gulf total averaged 19 percent for 1980–2006; 19 percent for the 1980–1996 baseline period; and 19, 18, and 18 percent for the 2000–2004, 2001–2005, and 2002–2006 5-year periods, respectively. Streamflow from the Missouri River Basin as a percentage of the to-the-Gulf

total averaged 12 percent for 1980–2006; 13 percent for the 1980–1996 baseline period; and 10, 9, and 9 percent for the 2000–2004, 2001–2005, and 2002–2006 5-year periods, respectively. Streamflow from the Arkansas River Basin as a percentage of the to-the-Gulf total averaged 6 percent for 1980–2006; 6 percent for the 1980–1996 baseline period; and 5, 5, and 4 percent for the 2000–2004, 2001–2005, and 2002–2006 5-year periods, respectively. Streamflow from the Red River Basin as a percentage of the to-the-Gulf total averaged 5 percent for 1980–2006; 5 percent for the 1980–1996 baseline period; and 5, 5, and 4 percent for the 2000–2004, 2001–2005, and 2002–2006 5-year periods, respectively (fig. 12). Hence,

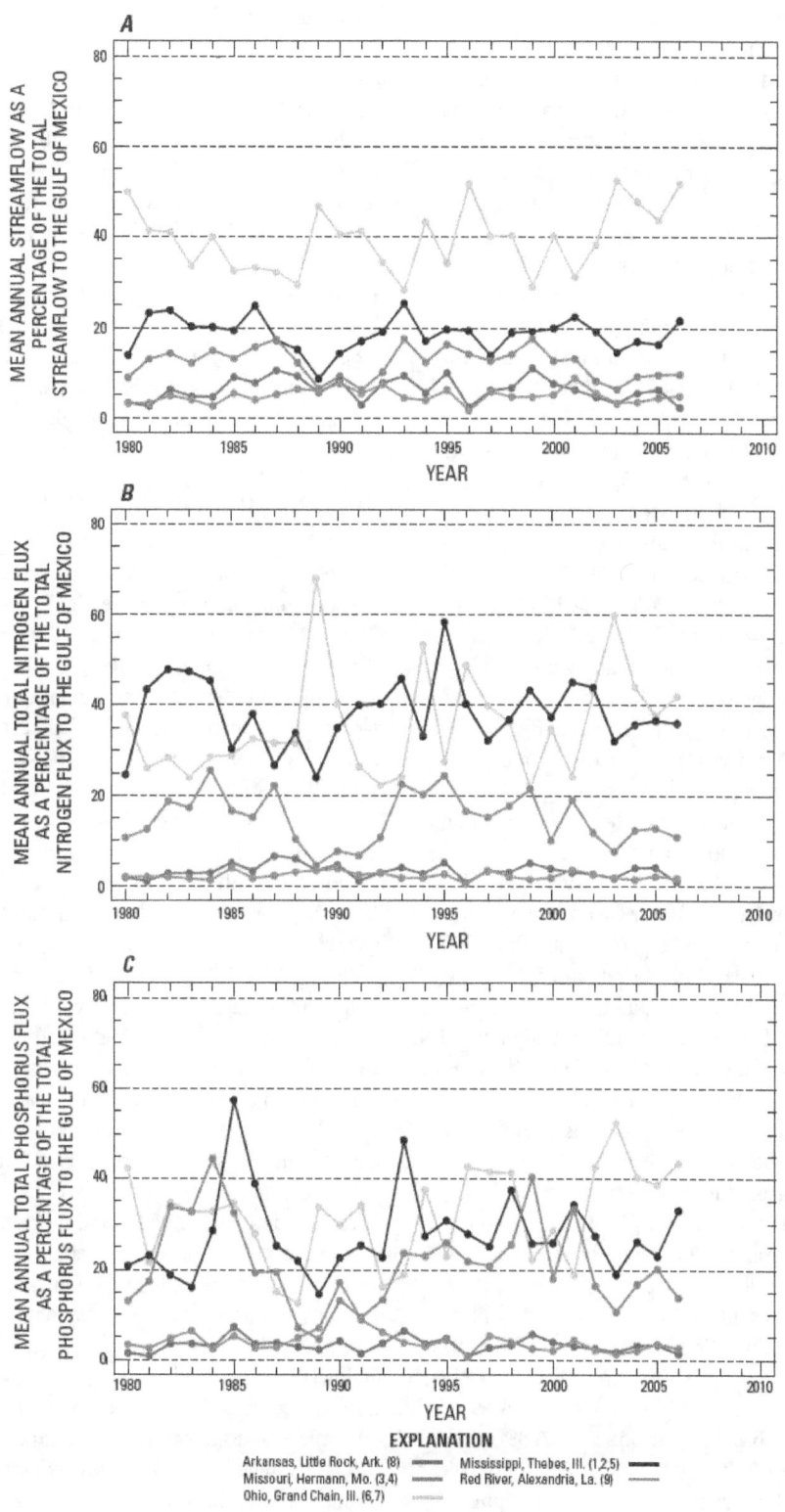

Figure 12. Mean annual (A) streamflow, (B) total nitrogen flux, and (C) total phosphorus flux from five major subbasins (numbers from figure 1) of the Mississippi-Atchafalaya River Basin, as a percentage of the total streamflow, total nitrogen, and total phosphorus flux in water delivered to the Gulf of Mexico.

the relative inputs of water from the major subbasins of the MARB has increased from the Ohio River Basin, decreased from the Missouri River Basin, and is relatively unchanged from the Upper Mississippi, Arkansas, and Red River Basins.

The sum of TN flux from the five subbasins as a percentage of total TN flux to the Gulf of Mexico ranged from 77 to 118 percent and averaged 95 percent for the 1980–2006 period. Values greater than 100 percent result from the assumption that no in-stream nutrient losses occur. TN fluxes from the Upper Mississippi and Ohio River Basins were generally larger than fluxes from the other three subbasins and averaged 38 and 36 percent of the to-the-Gulf total for 1980–2006, respectively. TN flux from the Upper Mississippi River Basin as a percentage of the to-the-Gulf total averaged 39 percent for the 1980–1996 baseline period and 39, 39, and 37 percent for the 2000–2004, 2001–2005, and 2002–2006 5-year periods, respectively. TN flux from the Ohio River Basin as a percentage of the to-the-Gulf total averaged 34 percent for the 1980–1996 baseline period and 41, 42, and 45 percent for the 2000–2004, 2001–2005, and 2002–2006 5-year periods, respectively. TN flux from the Missouri River Basin as a percentage of the to-the-Gulf total averaged 15 percent for 1980–2006; 16 percent for the 1980–1996 baseline period; and 12, 13, and 11 percent for the 2000–2004, 2001–2005, and 2002–2006 5-year periods, respectively. TN flux from the Arkansas River Basin as a percentage of the to-the-Gulf total averaged 6 percent for 1980–2006; 6 percent for the 1980–1996 baseline period; and 5, 5, and 4 percent for the 2000–2004, 2001–2005, and 2002–2006 5-year periods, respectively. TN flux from the Red River Basin as a percentage of the to-the-Gulf total averaged 5 percent for 1980–2006; 5 percent for the 1980–1996 baseline period; and 5, 5, and 4 percent for the 2000–2004, 2001–2005, and 2002–2006 5-year periods, respectively (fig. 12). Hence, the relative inputs of TN from the major subbasins of the MARB has increased from the Ohio River Basin, decreased from the Missouri River Basin, and is relatively unchanged from the Upper Mississippi, Arkansas, and Red River Basins.

The sum of TP flux from the five subbasins as a percentage of total TP flux to the Gulf of Mexico ranged from 50 to 137 percent, and averaged 88 percent for the 1980–2006 period. TP fluxes from the Ohio and Upper Mississippi River Basins were generally larger than fluxes from the other three subbasins and averaged 32 and 28 percent of the to-the-Gulf total for 1980–2006, respectively. TP flux from the Ohio River Basin as a percentage of the to-the-Gulf total averaged 29 percent for the 1980–1996 baseline period; and 37, 39, and 44 percent for the 2000–2004, 2001–2005, and 2002–2006 5-year periods, respectively. TP flux from the Upper Mississippi River Basin as a percentage of the to-the-Gulf total averaged 28 percent for the 1980–1996 baseline period; and 27, 26, and 26 percent for the 2000–2004, 2001–2005, and 2002–2006 5-year periods, respectively. TP flux from the Missouri River Basin as a percentage of the to-the-Gulf total averaged 21 percent for 1980–2006; 21 percent for the 1980–1996 baseline period; and 19, 20, and 16 percent for the 2000–2004,

2001–2005, and 2002–2006 5-year periods, respectively. TP flux from the Arkansas River Basin as a percentage of the to-the-Gulf total averaged 3 percent for 1980–2006; 3 percent for the 1980–1996 baseline period; and 3, 3, and 3 percent for the 2000–2004, 2001–2005, and 2002–2006 5-year periods, respectively. TP flux from the Red River Basin as a percentage of the to-the-Gulf total averaged 4 percent for 1980–2006; 5 percent for the 1980–1996 baseline period; and 2, 3, and 2 percent for the 2000–2004, 2001–2005, and 2002–2006 5-year periods, respectively (fig. 12). Hence, the relative inputs of TP from the major subbasins of the MARB has increased from the Ohio River Basin, decreased from the Missouri and Red River Basins, and is relatively unchanged from the Upper Mississippi and Arkansas River Basins.

Summary and Conclusions

Nutrients and freshwater delivered by the Mississippi and Atchafalaya Rivers drive algal production in the northern Gulf of Mexico, which results in the seasonal occurrence of hypoxic bottom waters along the Louisiana and Texas coast. In 1999, the U.S. Geological Survey estimated the flux of nitrogen, phosphorus, and silica at selected sites in the Mississippi Basin and to the Gulf of Mexico for 1980–1996. These flux estimates provided the baseline information used by the Mississippi River/Gulf of Mexico Watershed Nutrient Task Force to develop an Action Plan for reducing hypoxia in the northern Gulf of Mexico. The primary goal of the Action Plan was to achieve a reduction in the size (areal extent) of the hypoxic zone from an average of approximately 14,000 square kilometers in 1996-2000 to a 5-year moving average of less than 5,000 square kilometers by 2015.

Statistical models and adjusted maximum likelihood estimation using USGS Load Estimator (LOADEST) software were used to estimate annual and seasonal nutrient fluxes for 1980-2007 to the Gulf of Mexico and at selected sites on the Mississippi River and its tributaries. These data provide a means to evaluate the influence of natural and anthropogenic effects on delivery of water and nutrients to the Gulf of Mexico; to define subbasins that are the most important contributors of nutrients to the Gulf; and to investigate the relations among streamflow, nutrient fluxes, and the size and duration of the Gulf of Mexico hypoxic zone. A comparative analysis between the baseline period of 1980–1996 and 5-year moving averages thereafter indicate that the average annual streamflow and fluxes of silica, total nitrogen, nitrate, and orthophosphate to the Gulf of Mexico have decreased, whereas the flux of total phosphorus has increased. The average spring (April, May, and June) streamflow and fluxes of silica, total nitrogen, nitrate, and orthophosphate to the Gulf of Mexico also decreased, whereas the spring flux of total phosphorus has increased. Similar changes in streamflow and nutrient flux were observed at many sites within the basin. Most major inputs of nutrients in the Mississippi-Atchafalaya River Basin have increased or remained about the same. Annual inputs of nitrogen from fertilizer have increased from the 1980–1996 baseline period by about 12 percent, and annual inputs of phosphorus from fertilizer have increased by about 2 percent. Point-source inputs of nitrogen and phosphorus decreased, even though the human population in the basin increased.

Changes in streamflow and nutrient fluxes are related and temporal variations in sources of streamflow and nutrients complicate the interpretation of factors that affect nutrient delivery to the Gulf of Mexico. Parametric time-series models are used to separate natural variability in nutrient flux from changes due to other causes. Results indicate that the decrease in annual nutrient fluxes that has occurred between the 1980–1996 baseline period, and more recent years can largely be attributed to natural causes (climate and streamflow) and not management actions or other human controlled activities in the Mississippi-Atchafalya River Basin. Downward trends in total nitrogen, nitrate, ammonium, and orthophosphate that were detected at either the Mississippi River near St. Francisville, La., or the Atchafalaya River at Melville, La., occurred prior to 1995. In spite of the general decrease in nutrient flux, the average size of the Gulf of Mexico hypoxic zone has increased between 1997 and 2007. The reasons for this are not clear but could be due to the type or nature of nutrient delivery.

While the annual flux of total nitrogen to the Gulf of Mexico has decreased, the proportion of that flux that is nitrate has increased from about 55 percent in the 1980s to about 70 percent in recent years. The inputs of water (streamflow), total nitrogen, and total phosphorus from the major subbasins of the Mississippi-Atchafalaya River Basin as a percentage of the to-the Gulf totals have increased from the Ohio River Basin, decreased from the Missouri River Basin, and remained relatively unchanged from the Upper Mississippi, Red, and Arkansas River Basins.

References Cited

Alexander, R.B. and Smith, R.A., 1990, County-level estimates of nitrogen and phosphorus fertilizer use in the United States, 1945 to 1985: U.S. Geological Survey Open-File Report 1990–130. Accessed on 3/7/2007 at *http://pubs. usgs.gov/of/1990/ofr90130/*.

Alexander, R.B., Smith, R.A., Schwarz, G.E., Boyer, E.W., Nolan, J.V., and Brakebill, J.W., 2008, Differences in phosphorus and nitrogen delivery to the Gulf of Mexico from the Mississippi River Basin: Environmental Science and Technology, v. 42, p. 822–830.

Aulenbach, B.T., Buxton, H.T., and Battaglin, W.A., 2007, Streamflow and nutrient fluxes of the Mississippi-Atchafalaya River Basin and subbasins for the period of record through 2005: U.S. Geological Survey Open-File Report 2007–1080, available online at *http://toxics.usgs. gov/pubs/of-2007-1080/*.

Battaglin, W.A., and Goolsby, D.A., 1995, Spatial data in geographic information system format on agricultural chemical use, land use, and cropping practices in the United States: U.S. Geological Survey Water-Resources Investigations Report 1994–4176, 87 p.

Battaglin, W.A., and Goolsby, D.A., 1998, Regression models of herbicide concentrations in outflow from reservoirs in the Midwestern USA, 1992–1993: Journal of the American Water Resources Association, v. 34, no. 6, p. 1369–1390.

Boesch, D.F., Boynton, W.R., Crowder, L.B., Diaz, R.J., Howarth, R.W., Mee, L.D., Nixon, S.W., Rabalais, N.N., Rosenberg, R., Sanders, J.G., Scavia, D., and Turner, R.E., 2009, Nutrient enrichment drives Gulf of Mexico hypoxia: EOS, Transactions, American Geophysical Union, v. 90, no. 14, p. 117–118.

Booth, M.S., and Campbell, C., 2007, Spring nitrate flux in the Mississippi River Basin- A landscape model with conservation applications: Environmental Science and Technology, v. 41, no. 15, p. 5410–5418.

Burkart, M.R., and James, D.E., 1999, Agricultural-nitrogen contributions to hypoxia in the Gulf of Mexico: Journal of Environmental Quality, v. 28, p. 850–859.

Cohn, T.A., Caulder, D.L., Gilroy, E.J., Zynjuk, L.D., and Sommers, R.M., 1992, The validity of a simple statistical model for estimating fluvial constituent loads: An empirical study involving nutrient loads entering Chesapeake Bay. Water Resources Research, v. 28, 2352–2363.

Committee on Environment and Natural Resources, 2000, Integrated assessment of hypoxia in the Northern Gulf of Mexico: National Science and Technology Council Committee on Environment and Natural Resources, Washington, D.C., 58 p.

Committee on Environment and Natural Resources, 2003, An assessment of coastal hypoxia and eutrophication in U.S. Waters: National Science and Technology Council Committee on Environment and Natural Resources, Washington, D.C., 74 p.

Diaz, R.J., and Rosenberg, R., 2008, Spreading dead zones and consequences for marine ecosystems: Science, v. 321, no. 5891, p. 926–929.

Dodds, W.K., 2006, Nutrients and the "dead zone": the link between nutrient ratios and dissolved oxygen in the northern Gulf of Mexico: Frontiers in Ecology and the Environment, v. 4, no. 4, p. 211–217.

Donner, S.D., and Scavia, D., 2007, How climate controls the flux of nitrogen by the Mississippi River and the development of hypoxia in the Gulf of Mexico: Limnology and Oceanography, v. 52, no. 2, p. 856–861.

Ficke, J.F., and Hawkinson, R.O., 1975, The National Stream Accounting Network (NASQAN)—Some questions and answers: U.S. Geological Survey Circular 719, 23 p.

Goolsby, D.A., and Battaglin, W.A., 2000, Nitrogen in the Mississippi Basin—Estimating sources and predicting flux to the Gulf of Mexico: U.S. Geological Survey Fact Sheet 135–00, 4 p.

Goolsby, D.A., and Battaglin, W.A., 2001, Long-term changes in concentrations and flux of nitrogen in the Mississippi River Basin, USA: Hydrological Processes, v. 15, p. 1209–1226.

Goolsby, D.A., Battaglin, W.A., Lawrence, G.B., Artz, R.S., Aulenbach, B.T., Hooper, R.P., Keeney, D.R., and Stensland, G.J., 1999, Flux and sources of nutrients in the Mississippi-Atchafalaya River Basin topic 3 report for the integrated assessment on hypoxia in the Gulf of Mexico: Silver Spring, Maryland, NOAA Coastal Ocean Office, NOAA Coastal Ocean Program Decision Analysis Series no. 17, 130 p.

Goolsby, D.A., Battaglin, W.A., and Thurman, E.M., 1993. Occurrence and transport of agricultural chemicals in the Mississippi River Basin, July through August 1993: U.S. Geological Survey Circular 1120–C, 22 p.

Helsel, D.R. and Hirsh, R.M., 2002, Statistical methods in water resources: Techniques of Water-Resources Investigations of the United States Geological Survey, book 4, Hydrologic Analysis and Interpretation, chap. A3, 524 p. Accessed on 5/23/2008 at *http://www.practicalstats.com/aes/aesbook/files/HelselHirsch.PDF*.

Howarth, R.W., Boyer, E.W., Pabich, W.J., and Galloway, J.N., 2002, Nitrogen use in the United States from 1961-2000 and potential future trends: Ambio, v. 31, no. 2, p. 88–96.

Howarth, R.W., and Marino, R., 2006, Nitrogen as the limiting nutrient for eutrophication in coastal marine ecosystems—Evolving views over three decades: Limnology and Oceanography, v. 5. no. 1, p. 364–376.

Kolpin, D.W., Burkart, M.R., and Thurman, E.M., 1993, Hydrogeologic, water-quality and land-use data for the reconnaissance of herbicides and nitrate in near-surface aquifers of the midcontinental United States: U.S. Geological Survey Open-File Report 1993–114, 61 p.

Meade, R.H., 1995, Contaminants in the Mississippi River: U.S. Geological Survey Circular 1133, 140 p.

Mississippi River/Gulf of Mexico Watershed Nutrient Task Force, 2001, Action plan for reducing, mitigating, and controlling hypoxia in the Northern Gulf of Mexico: Washington, D.C., 31 p.

Mississippi River/Gulf of Mexico Watershed Nutrient Task Force, 2004, A science strategy to support management decisions related to hypoxia in the Northern Gulf of Mexico and excess nutrients in the Mississippi River Basin: Monitoring, Modeling, and Research Workgroup of the Mississippi River/Gulf of Mexico Watershed Nutrient Task Force, U.S. Geological Survey Circular 1270, 58 p. Accessed on 12/2008 at *http://pubs.usgs.gov/circ/2004/1270/*.

Mississippi River/Gulf of Mexico Watershed Nutrient Task Force, 2006, Reassessment of point source nutrient mass loading to the Mississippi River basin: U.S. Environmental Protection Agency, Mississippi River/Gulf of Mexico Watershed Nutrient Task Force, Management Action Reassessment Team, 31 p. Accessed on 4/30/2008 at *http://www.epa.gov/msbasin/taskforce/Point_Source_Mass_Loading.pdf*.

Mississippi River/Gulf of Mexico Watershed Nutrient Task Force, 2008, Gulf hypoxia action plan 2008 for reducing, mitigating, and controlling hypoxia in the Northern Gulf of Mexico and improving water quality in the Mississippi River Basin: Washington, D.C., 61 p.

Moody, J.A., 1993, Evaluation of the Lagrangian scheme for sampling the Mississippi River during 1987–1990: U.S. Geological Survey Water-Resources Investigations Report 1993–4042, 31 p.

Rabalais, N.N., Turner, R.E., Justic, D., Dortch, Q., and Wiseman, W.J., Jr., 1999, Characterization of Hypoxia: Topic 1 Report for the Integrated Assessment on Hypoxia in the Gulf of Mexico: Silver Spring, Maryland, NOAA Coastal Ocean Office, NOAA Coastal Ocean Program Decision Analysis Series n. 15, 167 p.

Rabalais, N.N., Turner, R.E., Dortch, Q., Justic, D., Beirman, V.J., and Wiseman, W.J., 2002, Nutrient-enhanced productivity in the Northern Gulf of Mexico—Past, present and future: Hydrobiologia, v. 176, p. 39–63.

Rabalais, N.N., Turner, R.E., Gupta, B.K., Boesch, D.F., Chapman, P., and Murrell, M.C., 2007, Hypoxia in the Northern Gulf of Mexico—Does the science support the plan to reduce, mitigate, and control hypoxia? Estuaries and Coasts, v. 30, no. 5, p. 753–772.

Rebich R.A., and Demcheck, D.K., 2007, Trends in nutrient and sediment concentrations and loads in major rivers basins of the south-central United States, 1993– 2004: U.S. Geological Survey Scientific Investigations Report 2007–5090, 112 p.

Ruddy, B.C., Lorenz, D.L., and Mueller, D.K., 2006, County-level estimates of nutrient inputs to the land surface of the conterminous United States, 1982–2001: U.S. Geological Survey Scientific Investigations Report 2006–5012. Accessed on 5/2006 at *http://pubs.usgs.gov/sir/2006/5012/*.

Runkel, R.L., Crawford, C.G., and Cohn, T.A., 2004, Load Estimator (LOADEST) —A FORTRAN program for estimating constituent loads in streams and rivers: U.S. Geological Survey Techniques and Methods book 4, chapter A5, online only at *http://pubs.usgs.gov/tm/2005/tm4A5*.

Scavia, D., and Donnelly, K.A., 2007, Reassessing hypoxia forecasts for the Gulf of Mexico: Environmental Science and Technology, v. 41, p. 8111–8117.

Scavia, D., Justic, D., and Bierman, V.J., 2004, Reducing hypoxia in the Gulf of Mexico—Advice from three models: Estuaries, v. 27, no. 3, p. 419–425.

Sprague, L.A., and Lorenz, D.L., 2009, Regional nutrient trends in streams and rivers of the United States, 1993-2003: Environmental Science and Technology, v. 43, no. 10, p. 3430–3479.

Stow, C.A., Qian, S.S., and Craig, J.K., 2005, Declining threshold for hypoxia in the Gulf of Mexico: Environmental Science and Technology, v. 39, no. 3, p. 716–723.

Sylvan, J.B., Dortch, Q., Nelson, D.M., Maier Brown, A.F., Morrison, W., and Ammerman, J.W., 2006, Phosphorus limits phytoplankton growth on the Louisiana shelf during the period of hypoxia formation: Environmental Science and Technology, v. 40, no. 24, p. 7548–7553.

Turner, R.E., Rabalais, N.N., and Justic, D., 2008, Gulf of Mexico hypoxia—Alternate states and a legacy: Environmental Science and Technology, v. 42, no. 7, p. 2322–2327, doi:10.1021/es071617k.

U.S. Census Bureau, 2008, Census 2000 Gateway. Accessed on 4/2008 at *http://www.census.gov/main/www.cen2000. html*.

U.S. Department of Agriculture, 2008, The Census of Agriculture: U.S. Department of Agriculture, National Agricultural Statistics Service. Accessed on 3/10/2008 at *http://www. agcensus.usda.gov/*.

U.S. Environmental Protection Agency, 2007, Hypoxia in the northern Gulf of Mexico—An update by the EPA Science Advisory Board: U.S. Environmental Protection Agency, EPA Science Advisory Board, EPA-SAB-08-003, accessed on 3/19/2008 at *http://yosemite.epa.gov/sab/sabproduct.nsf/ WebReportsOriginalStudyBOARD!OpenView*.

U.S. Environmental Protection Agency, 2008, Hypoxia in the Northern Gulf of Mexico—An update by the EPA Science Advisory Board: EPA Science Advisory Board, Washington, DC, EPA-SAB-08-003, 333 p, accessed on 12/2008 at *http://www.epa.gov/msbasin/pdf/sab_report_2007.pdf*.

U.S. Geological Survey, 1999, The quality of our Nation's waters—Nutrients and pesticides: U.S. Geological Survey Circular 1225, 82 p.

U.S. Geological Survey, 2009, USGS Hypoxia in the Gulf of Mexico Studies: U.S. Geological Survey Web site accessed on 7/2009 at *http://toxics.usgs.gov/hypoxia/*.

U.S. Geological Survey, variously dated, National field manual for the collection of water-quality data: U.S. Geological Survey Techniques of Water-Resources Investigations, book 9, chapters A1–A9, available online at *http://water.usgs.gov/ owq/FieldManual/*.

Vecchia, A.V., 2005, Water-quality trend analysis and sampling design for streams in the Red River of the North Basin, Minnesota, North Dakota, and South Dakota, 1970–2001: U.S. Geological Survey Scientific Investigations Report 2005–5224, 54 p.

Zhang, W.J., and Zhang, X.Y., 2007, A forecast analysis on fertilizers consumption worldwide: Environmental Monitoring and Assessment, v. 133, p. 427–434.